HIGH ADVENTURE crafts for Kids

**Includes Projects for Children
from Preschool to Sixth Grade:**

Colorful projects with a hot air ballooning theme!
Reproducible Awards and Certificates.
Bible Memory Verse Coloring Posters.

COMPILED BY KIM SULLIVAN

Gospel Light

How to Make Clean Copies from this Book

You may make copies of portions of this book with a clean conscience if:

■ you (or someone in your organization) are the original purchaser;

■ you are using the copies you make for a noncommercial purpose (such as teaching or promoting your ministry) within your church or organization;

■ you follow the instructions provided in this book.

However, it is ILLEGAL for you to make copies if:

■ you are using the material to promote, advertise or sell a product or service other than for ministry fund-raising;

■ you are using the material in or on a product for sale;

■ you or your organization are **not** the original purchaser of this book.

By following these guidelines you help us keep our products affordable.

Thank you,

Gospel Light

Library of Congress Cataloging-in-Publication Data
Sullivan, Kim.
   High adventure crafts for kids / compiled by Kim Sullivan.
   p. cm.
   Includes index.
   ISBN 0-8307-1851-6 (format-trade : alk. paper)
   1. Handicraft.   2. Hot air balloons in art.   3. Bible crafts.
   I. Gospel Light Publications (Firm)   II. Title.
   TT157.S843   1997
   745.5—dc20   96-35320
   CIP

William T. Greig, Publisher; **Dr. Elmer L. Towns,** Senior Consulting Publisher; **Billie Baptiste,** Publisher, Research, Planning and Development; **Christy Weir,** Senior Editor; **Kim Sullivan,** Associate Editor; **Linda Bossoletti,** Editorial Coordinator; **Linda Crisp, Neva Hickerson, Loreen Robertson, Dianne Rowell, Kim Sullivan,** Contributing Writers; **Aloyce Durrett, Sheryl Haystead, Neva Hickerson, Kathleen McIntosh, Barbara Morris, Loreen Robertson, Jonelle Stevens, Jan Worsham,** Contributing Editors; **Carolyn Thomas,** Designer; **Chizuko Yasuda,** Illustrator

Gospel Light

Contents

Introduction to High Adventure Crafts for Kids

Ballooning Fun

A hot air balloon festival fills the sky with excitement, color and wonder. Participants and observers alike enjoy the flurry of activity and atmosphere of fun preceding the balloon launch. When the colorful giants slowly rise from the ground they float silently over housetops, rivers and valleys, giving passengers a new view of the world below. The adventure of hot air ballooning is the inspiration behind the crafts of this resource book, *High Adventure Crafts for Kids*. Your students will catch the excitement as they create a kaleidoscope of colorful crafts.

In addition to learning about hot air balloons, your students will also explore the meaning of faith. Just as a hot air balloon rises in the sky, faith in God also takes us to new heights. Deciding to trust God and put our faith in Him allows us to experience life from a new perspective. Many of the crafts focus on the aspect of faith in the lives of your students as well as the lives of various people from the Bible.

We hope that you and your students will enjoy your flight of faith as you complete projects from *High Adventure Crafts for Kids*.

Personalize It!

We encourage you to use *High Adventure Crafts for Kids* as a basis for your craft program. You, as the teacher, parent or craft leader, play an essential role in leading enjoyable and successful craft projects for your children.

Feel free to alter the craft materials and instructions to suit your children's needs. Consider what materials you have on hand, what materials are available in your area and what materials you can afford to purchase. In some cases you will be able to substitute materials to use something you already have.

In addition, don't feel confined to the crafts in a particular age-level section. You may want to adapt a craft for younger and older age levels.

Three Steps to Success

What can you do to make sure craft time is successful and fun for your students? First, encourage creativity in each child! Remember, the process of creating is just as important as the final product. Provide a variety of materials with which children may work. Allow children to make choices on their own. Don't expect every child's project to turn out the same. Don't insist that children "stay in the lines."

Second, choose projects that are appropriate for the skill level of your students. Children become easily discouraged when a project is too difficult for them. Keep your children's skill level in mind when choosing craft projects. Finding the right projects for your students will increase the likelihood that all will be successful and satisfied with their finished products.

Finally, show an interest in the unique way each child approaches a project. Affirm the choices he or she has made. Treat each child's final product as a "masterpiece"!

The comments you give a child today can affect the way he or she views art in the future—so make it positive! Remember—the ability to create is part of being made in the image of God, the Creator!

Crafts with a Message

Many of the projects in *High Adventure Crafts for Kids* can easily become crafts with a message. Children can create slogans or poetry as part of their projects. Or, you may want to provide photocopies of an appropriate poem, thought or Bible verse for children to attach to their crafts. Here are some examples of ways to use verses and drawings to enhance the craft projects in this book.

"Trust in the Lord and do good. Commit your way to the Lord." Psalm 37:3,5

"Trust in the Lord and do good." Psalm 37:3

Be Prepared

If you are planning to use crafts with a child at home, here are three helpful tips:

❁ Focus on the crafts in the book designated for your child's age, but don't ignore projects that are listed for older or younger ages. Elementary-age children enjoy many of the projects geared for preschool and kindergarten children. And younger children are always interested in doing "big kid" things. Just plan on working along with the child, helping with tasks the child can't handle alone.

❁ Start with projects that call for materials you have around the house. Make a list of the items you do not have that are needed for projects you think your child will enjoy. Plan to gather those supplies in one expedition.

❁ If certain materials seem too difficult to obtain, a little thought can usually lead to appropriate substitutions. And often the homemade version ends up being an improvement over the original plan.

If you are planning to lead a group of children in doing craft projects, keep these hints in mind:

❁ Choose projects that will allow children to work with a variety of materials.

❁ Make your selection of all projects far enough in advance to allow time to gather all needed supplies in one coordinated effort. Many projects use some of the same items.

❁ Make up a sample of each project to be sure the directions are fully understood and potential problems can be avoided. **You may want to adapt some projects to simplify procedures or vary the materials required.**

❁ Many items can be acquired as donations from people or businesses if you plan ahead and make your needs known. Many churches distribute lists of materials needed to their congregations and community and are able to provide crafts at little or no cost. Some items can be brought by the children themselves.

❁ In making your supplies list, distinguish between items that every individual child will need and those that will be shared among a group.

❁ Keep in mind that some materials may be shared among more than one age level, but only if there is good coordination between the groups. It is extremely frustrating to a teacher to expect to have scissors, only to discover another group is using them. Basic supplies that are used repeatedly in craft projects should usually be provided to every group.

Pilot Briefing

Each craft in this book includes a very important section entitled *Pilot Briefing*. These sections are designed to help you enhance craft times with thought-provoking conversation that is age appropriate. The *Pilot Briefing* section for a project may relate to an aspect of faith, a Bible character or story of faith, or it may include interesting facts about piloting a hot air balloon. If your crafts program includes large groups of children, you may want to share these conversation suggestions with each helper who can in turn use them with individuals or small groups.

Craft Symbols

Many of the craft projects in *High Adventure Crafts for Kids* are appropriate for more than one age level. Next to the title of certain projects in this book you'll find the symbol shown to the right. This symbol tells what

projects are suitable or adaptable for all elementary-age children—first through sixth grades. As you select projects, consider the particular children you are working with. Feel free to use your own ideas to make projects simpler or more difficult depending on the needs of your students.

In addition, some craft projects in this book require less preparation than others. The symbol shown to the left tells which projects require minimal preparation.

Helpful Hints

Using Glue with Young Children

Since preschoolers have difficulty using glue bottles effectively, you may want to try one of the following procedures. Purchase glue in large containers (up to one gallon size).

a. Pour small amount of glue into several shallow containers (such as margarine tubs or the bottoms of soda bottles).

b. Dilute glue by mixing a little water into each container

c. Children use paste brushes to spread glue on project

OR

a. Pour a small amount of glue into a plastic margarine tub.

b. Give each child a cotton swab. The child dips the cotton swab into the glue and rubs glue on project.

c. Excess glue can be poured back into the large container at the end of each session.

Cutting with Scissors

When cutting with scissors is required for these crafts, take note of the fact that some of the children in your class may be left-handed. It is very difficult for a left-handed person to cut with scissors that were designed to be used with the right hand. Have available in your classroom two or three pairs of left-handed scissors. These can be obtained from a school supply center.

Using Acrylic Paints

Acrylic paints are required for many of the wood projects. Our suggestions are:

❀ Provide smocks or old shirts for your children to wear, as acrylics may stain clothes.

❀ Acrylics can be expensive for a large group of children To make paint go further, squeeze a small amount into a shallow container and add water until mixture has a creamy consistency. Or you may use acrylic house paints.

❀ Fill shallow containers with soapy water. Clean paintbrushes before switching colors and immediately after finishing project.

Crafts for Young Children

Craft projects for young children are a blend of, "I wanna do it myself!" and "I need help!" Each project, because it is intended to come out looking like a recognizable something, usually requires a certain amount of adult assistance—in preparing a pattern, in doing some cutting, in preselecting magazine pictures, in tying a knot, etc. The younger the child, the more the adult will need to do, but care must always be taken not to rob the child of the satisfaction of his or her own unique efforts. Neither must the adult's desire to have a nice finished project override the child's pleasure at experimenting with color and texture. Avoid the temptation to do the project for the child or to improve on the child's efforts.

Some of the crafts have enrichment and simplification ideas included with them. An enrichment idea provides a way to make the craft more challenging for the older child. A simplification idea helps the younger child complete the craft more successfully. If you find a child frustrated with some of the limitations of working on a structured craft—although most of the projects in this book allow plenty of leeway for children to be themselves—it may be a signal the child needs an opportunity to work with more basic, less structured materials: blank paper and paints, play dough, or abstract collages (gluing miscellaneous shapes or objects onto surfaces such as paper, cardboard or anything else to which glue will adhere). Remember the cardinal rule of thumb in any task a young child undertakes: The process the child goes through is more important than the finished product.

Paper Plate Balloon

(25-30 MINUTES)

Materials: Colored poster board, hole punch, colored felt pens, small stickers (stars, hearts, circles or other shapes), glue, scissors, ruler, ribbon or rickrack scraps, ⅛-inch (.3125-cm) ribbon. For each child—two large sturdy white paper plates.

Preparation: For each child, glue the rims of two paper plates together with the front of plates facing to the inside (sketch a). With hole punch, punch a hole in the rim of glued paper plates at the top center. Punch two holes on the bottom rim, 3 inches (7.5 cm) apart (sketch b). Cut poster board into 3x3-inch (7.5x7.5-cm) squares—one square for each child. Punch two holes on one edge of each poster board square. Cut ⅛-inch (.3125-cm) ribbon into 12-inch (30-cm) and 6-inch (15-cm) lengths—one length of each size for each child.

Instruct each child in the following procedures:

❀ Color both sides of paper plate balloon with felt pens.

❀ Glue on ribbon scraps for balloon stripes.

❀ Decorate balloon with stickers.

❀ Use ribbon, stickers or felt pens to decorate poster board square as the balloon basket.

❀ Thread longer length of ⅛-inch (.3125-cm) ribbon through holes at the bottom of balloon plate, then thread through holes in poster board square. With teacher's help, tie ribbon ends together (sketch c).

❀ Thread shorter length of ⅛-inch (.3125-cm) ribbon through hole at the top of plate. Tie the ends together to form a hanging loop.

Pilot Briefing: (Shandra), what fills up a real balloon? (Air.) **A hot air balloon floats in the sky because it has hot air inside it. Hot air rises so it lifts up the balloon. The balloon pilot heats up the air inside the balloon with blasts of flames from a burner. What can you name that is hot? What things are really cold?**

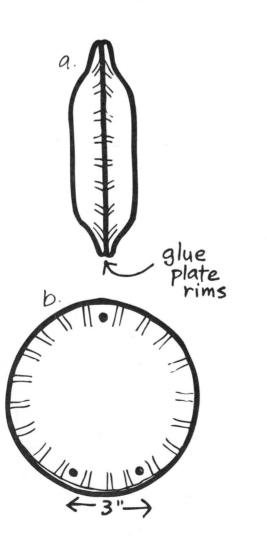

a.

glue plate rims

b.

← 3" →

c.

tie

tie

8

Balloon Glow Picture

(25-30 MINUTES)

Materials: Colored tissue paper, liquid starch, sponge brushes, pencil, ruler, burlap, yarn, cotton balls, scissors, glue, transparent tape, shallow containers, newspaper. For each child—one clear overhead transparency, one large sheet of blue construction paper.

Preparation: Draw a large balloon pattern onto each sheet of construction paper and cut out interior of balloon, leaving the rest of the paper intact (sketch a). Cut yarn into 3-inch (7.5-cm) lengths—four for each child. Cut tissue paper into 1 ½-inch (3.75-cm) squares. Cut burlap into 3-inch (7.5-cm) squares—one for each child. Pour liquid starch into shallow containers. Cover work area with newspaper.

Instruct each child in the following procedures:

❀ Use sponge brush to paint liquid starch over a section of the transparency.

❀ Put squares of colored tissue onto starched area, then gently paint over tissue with more starch, smoothing down any wrinkles.

❀ Continue covering the transparency with tissue and starch, overlapping squares. Leave an uncovered border of about 1 inch (2.5 cm). Let dry.

❀ On the front of picture, glue yarn hanging from balloon for ropes.

❀ Glue burlap square to ropes for basket.

❀ Gently pull cotton balls apart to make clouds and glue to picture for clouds.

❀ With teacher's help, carefully tape transparency to construction paper, with the tissue side of transparency showing through the balloon cutout (sketch b).

❀ Tape your picture in a window to see your colorful hot air balloon glow.

Enrichment Ideas: Take a photo of each child, develop film and cut out child's image. Glue child's photo in balloon basket. Add hot air balloon stickers in the sky.

Pilot Briefing: What colors are on your balloon, (Rachel)? What is your favorite color? What has God made that is (yellow)? God has made beautiful things for us to see in so many different colors!

a. cut out balloon shape

b. tape onto construction paper

Balloon Brigade Window Decals

(10-15 MINUTES)

Materials: Up, Up and Away Balloon Pattern (p.13), white glue in squeeze bottles, food coloring, small mixing bowls, spoon, funnels, copier paper, photocopier, masking tape. For each child—one clear overhead transparency.

Preparation: Make colored glue by pouring glue into bowls and adding a few drops of food coloring. Mix several different colors in bowls. Use funnel to pour glue back into squeeze bottles. Photocopy Balloon Pattern (p. 13) onto paper—one copy for each child.

Instruct each child in the following procedures:

❁ With teacher's help, tape hot air balloon photocopy onto table. Tape transparency directly over photocopy (sketch a).

❁ Squeeze colored glue over the photocopied balloon shape onto transparency. Use different colors to make designs. Completely fill in balloon shape with a thick layer of glue (sketch b).

❁ Allow glue to dry overnight.

❁ With teacher's help, gently peel balloon shape from transparency.

❁ Children stick their balloons on a classroom window to make a colorful balloon brigade.

Simplification Idea: Purchase premade colored glue in squeeze bottles.

Enrichment Idea: Children use Weather Patterns on p. 20 to make additional decal shapes.

Pilot Briefing: **(Jordan), what would happen if you didn't listen to the directions for making your balloon?** (I wouldn't know what to do. It might not turn out right.) **Because you listen and follow directions, your balloon decal will be very bright and beautiful! God wants you to follow His directions in the Bible. He also wants you to follow your parent's directions and obey them. What are some things you can do to obey your mom or dad?**

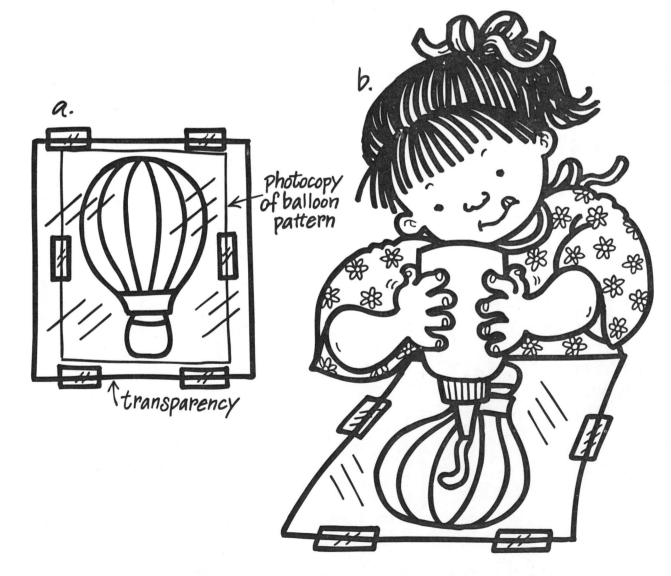

Colored-Pebble Balloon Frame

(20-25 MINUTES)

Materials: Balloon Mobile Pattern (p. 34), camera, film, scissors, craft knife, sturdy poster board, small aquarium pebbles in a variety of bright colors, bottles of glue, hole punch, shallow containers, transparent tape.

Preparation: The day before craft, take a horizontal photo of each child standing in front of a blue or sky background. Photograph child from the waist up. Develop film same day. Trace Balloon Mobile Pattern onto poster board and cut out—one for each child. With craft knife, cut out opening for photo on each balloon. Punch a hole at the top of poster board balloons. Pour colored pebbles into shallow containers—one container for each color.

Instruct each child in the following procedures:

❀ With teacher's help, squeeze thick lines of glue from the top of balloon to the bottom to make balloon stripes (sketch a).

❀ Place colored pebbles on glue lines to fill in stripes. Make each stripe a different color.

❀ With teacher's help, squeeze glue on balloon basket (sketch b).

❀ Place pebbles on glued basket. Let dry.

❀ With teacher's help, tape photo to the back of poster board at opening, trimming photo edges where needed.

Enrichment Idea: Older children may make their own designs with glue on the balloon and basket, then cover with pebbles.

Pilot Briefing: **(Tony,) does your balloon frame feel heavy or light with all the pebbles on it?** (Heavy.) **A real hot air balloon is very light. The hot air inside the balloon lifts it up into the sky. What are some things that are light? What things are heavy?**

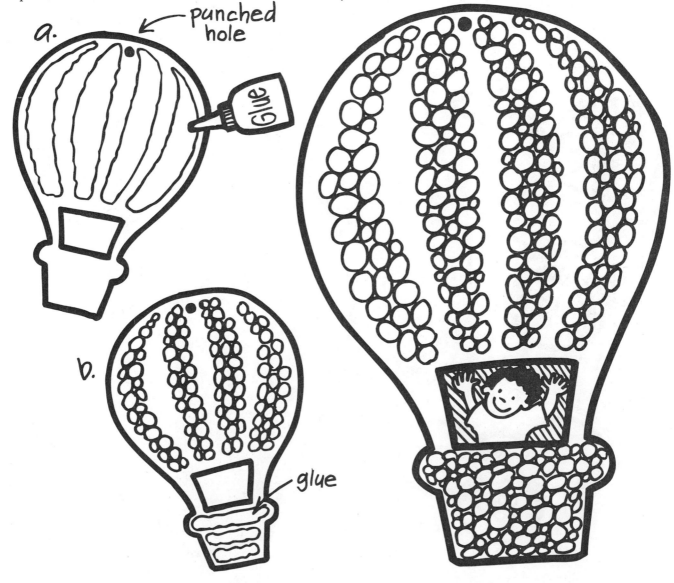

a.

punched hole

Glue

b.

glue

BuSy Bee Balloon

(20-25 MINUTES)

Materials: Bee Wing Pattern, yellow card stock, pencil, hole punch, transparent tape, wide-tip black permanent felt pens, black chenille wires, black yarn, scissors, measuring stick. For each child—one round yellow balloon.

Preparation: Use Bee Wing Pattern to trace onto card stock—two wings for each child. Cut out wings. Cut chenille wires in half—one half for each child. Cut yarn into 1-yard (90-cm) lengths—one for each child. Inflate balloons to approximately 5 inches (12.5 cm) in diameter.

Instruct each child in the following procedures:

❋ With felt pen, draw a large circle on the top of balloon for the bee's face (sketch a).

❋ Draw eyes, eyebrows, nose and mouth in the circle.

❋ Draw wide stripes around the balloon to make the bee's body.

❋ With hole punch, punch a hole in the round end of each wing.

❋ Fold the straight edge of each wing down ½ inch (1.25 cm).

❋ With teacher's help, tape the wings to the sides of the bee body. Tape underneath the wing, then on top of the wing to secure (sketch b).

❋ With teacher's help, thread the yarn through hole in wing and tie in a knot. Repeat with the opposite end of yarn. Tie a knot in the middle of yarn to make loop for holding or hanging (sketch c).

❋ Bend chenille wire into a U-shape. Bend the tips of wire to make antennae. Tape the antennae to the top of the bee's face (sketch c).

Enrichment Ideas: Older children may cut out their own bee wings. Children may glue gold, clear or yellow sequins to the wings.

Pilot Briefing: **What sound does a bee make, (Kyle)? Where do you see bees? Bees keep busy outside in gardens where there are lots of flowers. They gather their food from the flowers and take it back to the beehive, where they make it into honey. God made the flowers so that the bees have food to eat. He made the bees so people and animals have honey to eat. What other good things has God made that you like to eat?**

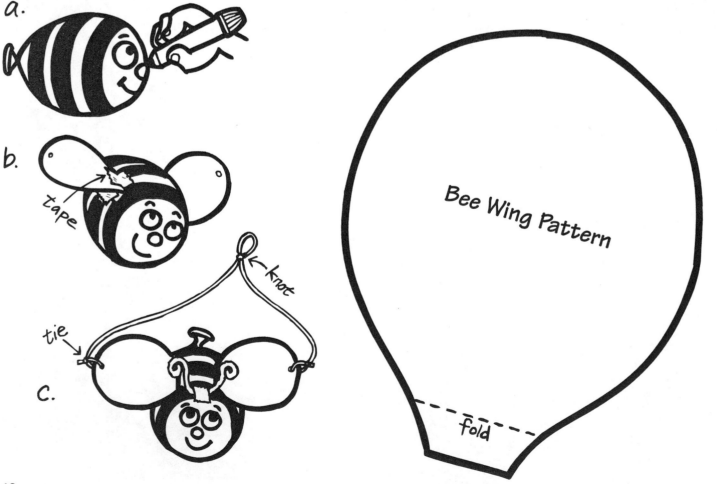

a.

b. tape

c. tie / knot

Bee Wing Pattern

fold

Up, Up and Away

(TWO-DAY CRAFT/20 MINUTES TOTAL TIME)

Materials: Up, Up and Away Balloon Pattern, white tagboard, pencil, tempera paints in various bright colors, corn syrup, paintbrushes, bright-colored embroidery floss, scissors, measuring stick, hole punch, shallow containers, newspaper, disposable wipes. For each child—three ½-inch (1.25-cm) wooden beads.

Preparation: Trace Balloon Pattern onto tagboard and cut out—one balloon for each child. Punch six holes in balloon as shown in sketch a. Cut embroidery floss into 4-foot (1.2-m) lengths—one for each child. Cover work area with newspaper. Pour paint into shallow containers.

DAY ONE

Instruct each child in the following procedures:

❀ Teacher pours a drop of corn syrup on the center of the balloon.

❀ With paintbrush, add paint to corn syrup to make shiny paint. Use fingers or paintbrush to mix paint and spread mixture around balloon shape. Allow paint to dry overnight.

❀ Use disposable wipes to clean hands.

DAY TWO

Instruct each child in the following procedures:

❀ Fold embroidery floss in half. With teacher's help, thread folded floss through bead (sketch b). Slide bead down about 3 inches (7.5 cm).

❀ With teacher's help, tie a double knot above bead leaving loop at top for hanging (sketch b).

❀ Thread one end of floss through punched holes on one side of balloon as shown in sketch c. Repeat with other end of string on opposite side of balloon.

❀ Thread a bead on each end of string. With teacher's help, tie a double knot below each bead.

❀ Place loop around doorknob or other hook. Slide balloon up and down strings to make your balloon "take off" or "land."

Pilot Briefing: **(Karina), how do you think it would feel to go up, up in the sky in a hot air balloon?** (Child responds.) **Some people might be afraid to be high in the sky. Some people might think it is fun to be up in the clouds. Wherever we are, we can know that God is always with us. The Bible says, "Do not be afraid...God is with you."** (See Deuteronomy 31:6.)

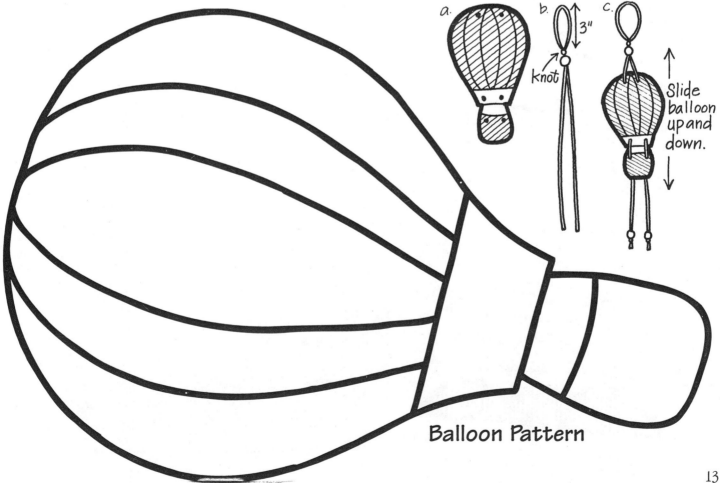

Balloon Pattern

Sky-High Travel Tote

(20-25 MINUTES)

Materials: Light blue acrylic spray paint, white and yellow acrylic paint, sponges, prepasted wallpaper scraps in green and tan small prints, water, sponge brushes, scissors, hot air balloon stickers, ¼-inch (.625-cm) cording, ruler, ice pick or awl, pie tins, shallow containers, newspaper. For each child—one clean laundry detergent box (approximately 5x8½x8½-inch [12.5x21.5x21.5-cm]) with flip-top lid.

Preparation: With ice pick, poke holes on the opposite sides of each box, 1½ inches (3.75 cm) from the top edge (sketch a). Widen hole to about a ¼-inch (.625-cm) opening. Spray boxes with blue spray paint. Cut green and tan wallpaper into hill shapes with a straight edge at the bottom (sketch b). Cut damp sponges into cloud shapes and round suns. Cut cording into 2-foot (60-cm) lengths—one for each child. Pour white and yellow paint into pie tins. Pour water into shallow containers. Cover work area with newspaper.

Instruct each child in the following procedures:

❀ With sponge brush, brush water onto the back of wallpaper mountain and hill shapes to activate wallpaper paste.

❀ Place wallpaper shapes at the bottom of each side of the box to make the land (sketch c). Smooth wallpaper down.

❀ Press cloud-shaped sponge in white paint. Then press sponge onto the blue part of box to make a cloud. Repeat sponging to make clouds on every side of box.

❀ Press circle sponge in yellow paint and then press onto box to make a sun in the sky. Allow paint to dry.

❀ Place hot air balloon stickers in the sky.

❀ For carrying handle, poke the cording into one of the holes on the side of the box and pull through to the inside. With teacher's help, tie a large knot at the end of cording inside the box to secure. Repeat for the other hole.

Enrichment Idea: Older children may cut out their own wallpaper mountain and hill shapes. They may cut out wallpaper house and tree shapes to add to their landscape.

Pilot Briefing: **There are many things you can do with your travel tote. You can carry things that are special to you. You can use your tote to hold your Bible and other books. You can even carry home the special things you make at VBS! What will you put in your travel tote, (Eric)?**

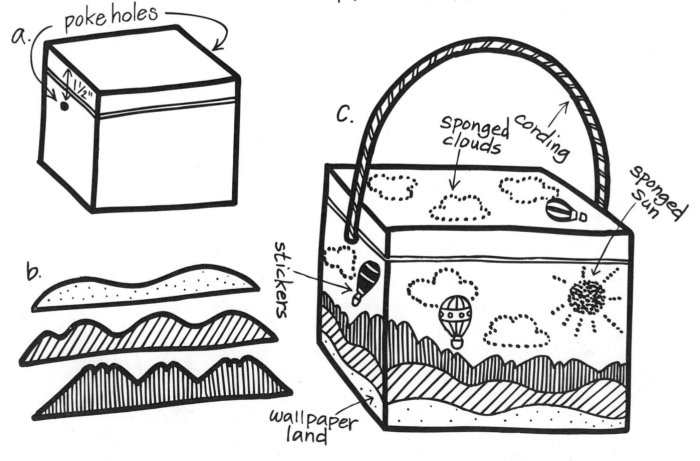

a. poke holes 1½"

b.

c. sponged clouds cording sponged sun stickers wallpaper land

Rainbow Glass Vase

(20-25 MINUTES)

Materials: Craft tissue paper in various colors, scissors, liquid starch, shallow containers, ruler, sponge brushes, clear acrylic spray, newspaper. For each child—one small, glass soda or water bottle.

Preparation: Cut tissue paper into 1½-inch (3.75-cm) squares. Pour liquid starch into shallow containers. Cover work area with newspaper.

Instruct each child in the following procedures:

❀ Paint starch onto the outside of the glass bottle.

❀ Lay tissue paper squares on top of starch.

❀ Gently paint more starch on top of tissue and smooth out any wrinkles.

❀ Cover the bottle completely, overlapping tissue. Let dry.

❀ In a well-ventilated area, teacher sprays vases with clear acrylic spray.

Pilot Briefing: **Your Rainbow Vase has many pretty colors on it, just like a rainbow! What colors are in a rainbow, (Justine)? God made the rainbow in the sky. Every time you see a rainbow you can remember that He loves you and made you, too!**

Snowball Soap Surprises

(10-15 MINUTES)

Materials: Ivory Snow detergent, water pitcher, water, measuring cup and spoons. For each child—one margarine tub or small bowl, plastic spoon, small plastic animal or toy figure (such as math counters found in school supply stores), plastic sandwich bag.

Preparation: Fill pitcher with water.

Instruct each child in the following procedures:

❀ Measure ½ cup detergent and pour into bowl.

❀ Teacher measures 1½ teaspoon water and adds to the detergent.

❀ Mix soap with spoon. Then knead mixture with your hands. Teacher adds more water by the half-teaspoonfuls if needed.

❀ Mold soap mixture around small toy figure. Smooth soap into a ball. Let dry to harden.

❀ Take home soap ball in sandwich bag. Use soap in the bathtub or to wash hands.

Enrichment Idea: Have children make more than one soap ball and give one to a friend.

Pilot Briefing: **Do you like surprises? When was a time you were surprised by something special, (Daniel)? A long time ago, Jesus' friends were surprised when something very special happened. An angel told them that Jesus was alive! They were so happy! Jesus is still alive today. He is God's Son, and He loves you and me!**

Drip-Drop Raindrop Game

(25-30 MINUTES)

Materials: Raindrop Weather Pattern (p. 20), pencil, acrylic paints in rainbow colors, paintbrushes, kitchen sponges, sharp scissors, glue, white heavy-weight poster board, wide-tip colored felt pens, shallow containers, clear acrylic spray, newspaper. For each child—one plastic gallon-sized milk jug.

Preparation: Using Raindrop Pattern, trace onto poster board and cut out 12 raindrops for each child. Cut a large opening in the top of each milk jug, leaving the handle intact (sketch a)—one for each child. Dampen sponges. Cut sponges into cloud shapes. Pour paint into containers. Cover work area with newspaper.

Instruct each child in the following procedures:
* With paintbrush, paint a rainbow on the jug.
* Paint a yellow sun.
* Dip cloud-shaped sponge into blue paint and print several clouds on the jug (sketch b).
* Let jug dry.
* Use felt pens to color one set of six poster board raindrops one color.
* Glue two raindrops together, colored sides facing out. Repeat to make three double-thick raindrops.
* Color second set of six raindrops using a different color. Glue to make three double-thick raindrops.
* In a well-ventilated area, teacher sprays milk jugs with clear acrylic spray. Let dry.
* *To play with a friend:* Set jug on the floor. Each player stands the same distance from the jug holding one set of raindrops. Taking turns, they try to toss raindrops into the jug.

Enrichment Idea: Fill small balloons with a small amount of water or sand and tie. Make six filled balloons (three each of two different colors) for each child. Children use balloons as raindrop game pieces instead of poster board raindrops.

Pilot Briefing: **You can play your Raindrop Game with a friend. Who is a friend you like to play with, (Jackie)? (Child responds.) Jesus is your friend, too. He loves you. You can learn about Jesus when you listen to Bible stories. You can talk to Him when you pray. Jesus cares about you very much.**

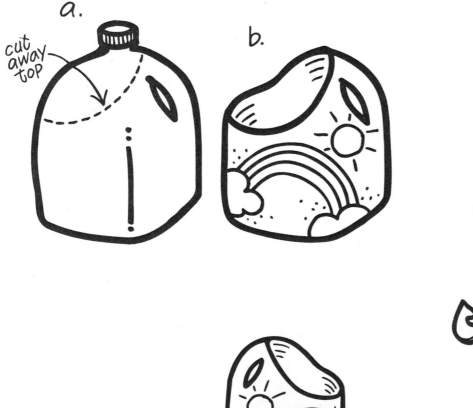

Breeze Catcher

(25-30 MINUTES)

Materials: Sun Pattern, yellow construction paper, white butcher paper, lightweight cardboard, measuring stick, pencil, blue chalk, paper towels, crepe paper streamers in red, orange, yellow, green, blue, and purple, scissors, white glue or glue sticks, hole punch, aerosol hair spray, yarn. Optional—stapler and staples.

Preparation: Trace Sun Pattern onto yellow construction paper and cut out—one sun for each child. Draw a large pattern of a cloud, approximately 14x17 inches (35x42.5 cm), onto lightweight cardboard and cut out. Using cardboard pattern, trace and cut out two butcher paper clouds for each child. Cut crepe paper streamers into 18-inch (45-cm) lengths—one length of each color for each child. Cut yarn into 16-inch (40-cm) lengths— one for each child.

Instruct each child in the following procedures:

* Color paper clouds with blue chalk.
* In well-ventilated area, with teacher's help, spray the clouds with hair spray to set chalk.
* Lay one paper cloud with colored side down.
* Glue one end of each crepe paper streamer across the bottom of cloud in rainbow-color order (red, orange, yellow, green, blue, and purple (sketch a).
* Lay the second cloud with the colored side down and apply glue around the edge of the cloud, leaving a 6-inch (15-cm) opening near the top (sketch b).
* Place the glued cloud on top of the cloud with streamers, colored side up. Making sure edges are even, press glued edges together firmly (sketch b).
* Scrunch up 3 or 4 paper towels and gently stuff into the opening near the top of cloud.
* Glue opening closed.
* Glue paper sun onto top corner of cloud.
* Punch two holes near the top of the cloud, about 4 inches (10 cm) apart. Thread with yarn for hanging and tie a knot at ends (sketch c).

Simplification Idea: Teacher uses stapler to staple edges of clouds together for children.

Pilot Briefing: You can hang your Breeze Catcher near an open window to see the streamers flutter in the wind. Many things float or fly in the wind. What can you name that floats or flies in the wind? (Hot air balloons, birds, airplanes, leaves, balloons, etc.)

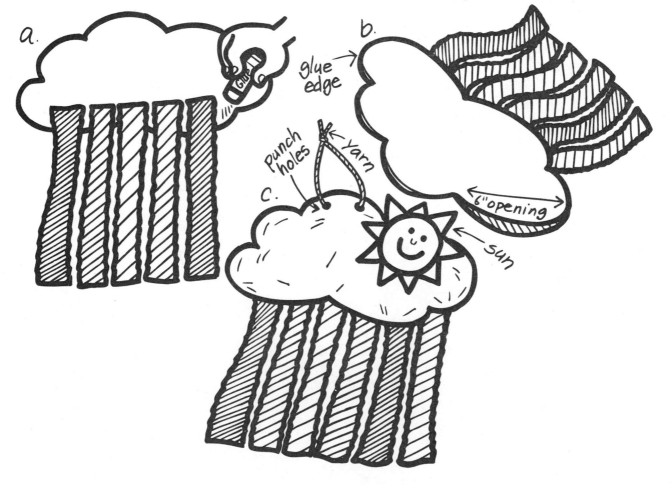

Sun Pattern

Weather Wheel

**(ONE- OR TWO-DAY CRAFT/
25-35 MINUTES TOTAL TIME)**

Materials: Weather Patterns on p. 20 (raindrop, lightning bolt, cloud, sun and house), old sponges, tempera paint in a variety of colors including blue and green, felt pens, shallow containers, spring-type clothespins, old blunt pencils with eraser tops, felt in a variety of colors including white, grey, light blue and yellow, yarn, craft knife, ruler, hole punch, glue, scissors, newspaper. For each child—two large, sturdy white paper plates, 1-inch (2.5-cm) paper fastener, one pony bead.

DAY ONE

Preparation: With the pointed tip of craft knife, poke a small hole in the center of each paper plate. In half of the plates, use craft knife to cut out a pie-shaped window 1 inch (2.5 cm) above hole (sketch a). With pencil, draw a line for horizon (sketch a). Dampen and cut sponges into 1-inch (2.5-cm) pieces. Clip a clothespin to each sponge to use as a handle. Pour paint into shallow containers. Cover work area with newspaper.

Instruct each child in the following procedures:

❀ Sponge paint the entire front of uncut plate with blue paint. Set aside and let dry.

❀ On the front of the other plate, sponge paint the window portion blue for sky (sketch b).

❀ Sponge paint the bottom portion of plate green for grass.

❀ Sponge paint the rim of plate any color.

❀ Dip eraser end of pencil into paint and press on grass several times to make flowers. Repeat with desired colors.

DAY TWO

Preparation: Trace Weather Patterns onto felt and cut out blue raindrops, yellow suns, grey lightning bolts, white clouds and any color house—one of each shape for each child.

Instruct each child in the following procedures:

❀ Glue felt weather cut-outs onto solid blue plate. Space evenly around plate (sketch c).

❀ Glue felt house onto window plate and decorate with felt pens or felt scraps.

❀ Punch hole in top of window plate. With teacher's help, cut and tie yarn through hole.

❀ With teacher's help, assemble plates. Poke paper fastener through the center front of window plate. Thread a pony bead on the shank of fastener, then poke fastener into center front of second plate and bend fastener to secure in back (sketch d). Bead will keep plates spaced apart.

❀ Turn bottom plate to view the four weather shapes.

Simplification: Use paper instead of felt for weather cutouts.

Pilot Briefing: **(Eric), what do you like to do when it is (sunny, rainy, cloudy, etc.)? You can turn your Weather Wheel to show the (sun). God gives us rain, snow and sun. God knows what our world needs to make plants, animals and people grow.**

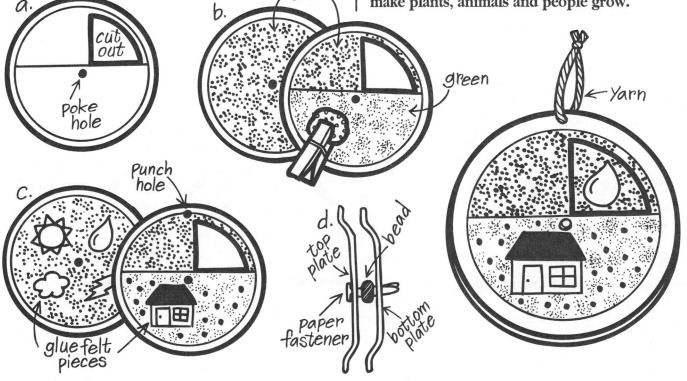

a. cut out / poke hole

b. blue / green

c. Punch hole / glue felt pieces

d. top plate / paper fastener / bead / bottom plate

yarn

Weather Patterns

Raindrop

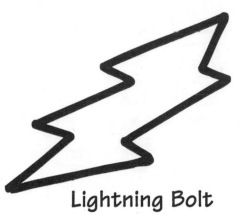

Lightning Bolt

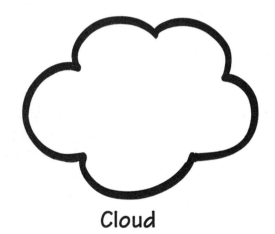

Cloud

Sun

House

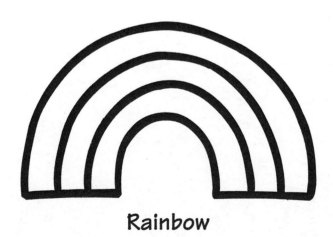

Rainbow

Weather Hat

**(ONE- OR TWO-DAY CRAFT/
35-45 MINUTES TOTAL TIME)**

Materials: Weather Patterns on p. 20 (sun, lightning bolt, rainbow, raindrop), poster board in white, blue and yellow, scissors, colored felt pens, silver glitter, glue, measuring stick, pencil, craft knife, tempera paint in light blue, green, purple and yellow, shallow containers, wide and thin paintbrushes, newspaper, blue curling ribbon, ¼-inch silver mylar ribbon (found with gift wrapping supplies), stapler and staples, cotton balls, snowflake confetti or sequins. For each child—one sturdy white 10-inch (25-cm) paper plate.

DAY ONE

Preparation: Use ruler and pencil to divide the bottom of paper plates into eight even wedges (sketch a). With craft knife, cut wedges apart on pencil lines leaving a 1- to 2-inch (2.5- to 5-cm) uncut rim (sketch a). Pour paint into shallow containers. Cover work area with newspaper.

Instruct each child in the following procedures:

❀ Lay paper plate upside down. Paint the cut portion of the plate blue for sky.

❀ Use wide paintbrush to paint the rim of the plate green for grassy hills (sketch b).

❀ With thin paintbrush, dot purple and yellow flowers on grass. Let paint dry.

DAY TWO

Preparation: Trace Weather Patterns onto poster board. Cut out one yellow sun, one white lightning bolt, one white rainbow and four blue raindrops for each child. Cut

curling ribbon and mylar ribbon into 18-inch (45-cm) lengths—four lengths of blue ribbon and five lengths of mylar ribbon for each child.

Instruct each child in the following procedures:

❀ Glue a blue raindrop to one end of each blue ribbon.

❀ Glue silver glitter onto white lightning bolt.

❀ Color rainbow with felt pens.

❀ Lay paper plate with paint side up. Bend blue sky wedges up (sketch c).

❀ On bent up wedges, glue the colored rainbow, lightning bolt and yellow sun.

❀ Glue cotton balls on sky for clouds.

❀ Glue snowflake confetti or sequins on the sky.

❀ With teacher's help, staple the free ends of blue ribbon and mylar ribbon onto one half of the hat rim. Alternate blue and mylar ribbons and space evenly (sketch d).

❀ Try on your weather hat!

Enrichment Idea: Make a weather mobile by attaching four 2-foot (.6-cm) strings evenly around the plate and tying together to make a hanger.

Pilot Briefing: **Our world needs all kinds of weather. Why do we need rain?** (It gives people, animals and plants water to drink. Rain fills our lakes and oceans.) **Why do we need sun?** (It keeps us warm, gives us light, makes plants grow.) **Who made the rain and sun?** (God.) **What other things do you see on your weather hat that God has made?**

a. cut here

b. green blue

purple and yellow flowers

c. bend up wedges

d.

"Part-the-Water" Picture

(20-25 MINUTES)

Materials: Tan and blue acrylic paint, sponges, spring-type clothespins, brown and orange construction paper, colored dot label stickers, yarn, hole punch, glue sticks, pencil, ruler, scissors, shallow containers, newspaper. For each child—one 8½x11-inch (21.5x27.5-cm) sheet of white card stock, one overhead transparency.

Preparation: Draw a pencil line horizontally across the center of each sheet of card stock and transparency (sketch a). Cut brown construction paper into wavy mountain range shape approximately 2x11 inches (5x27.5 cm)—one for each child (sketch b). Cut orange construction paper into 1½-inch (3.75-cm) circles—one for each child. Cut damp sponges into small squares—one for each child. Clip a clothespin to each sponge. Cover work area with newspaper. Pour paint into shallow containers.

Instruct each child in the following procedures:

❋ Use tan paint to sponge paint bottom half of white card stock (sketch c).

❋ Use blue paint to sponge paint bottom half of transparency. Allow paint to dry.

❋ Use glue stick to glue mountain range above tan section on card stock (sketch d).

❋ Use glue stick to glue orange sun above mountains.

❋ Stick dot labels in the middle of tan section to represent the Israelites crossing the dry ground.

❋ Lay transparency on top of paper so that the blue paint is covering the tan paint. With teacher's help, use hole punch to punch four evenly-spaced holes along both sides of card stock and transparency (sketch e).

❋ With teacher's help, insert yarn through first hole and tie a knot. Thread yarn through remaining holes as shown in sketch e and tie another knot to secure. Repeat process for opposite edge of picture.

❋ Teacher uses scissors to cut transparency in half vertically (sketch f).

❋ Open and close top sheet to show how God parted the Red Sea and allowed the Israelites to cross on dry ground.

Enrichment Idea: Older children may draw happy faces on dots with fine-tip felt pens.

Simplification Idea: Use Bible character stickers for Moses and the Israelites.

Pilot Briefing: **God took care of the Israelites when they escaped from Egypt. He wanted them to travel safely to a new home. How did God help them escape when they reached the Red Sea?** (God sent a big wind that blew the sea back. Then the people could walk across to the other side.) **What do you think the Israelites said after God helped them escape?**

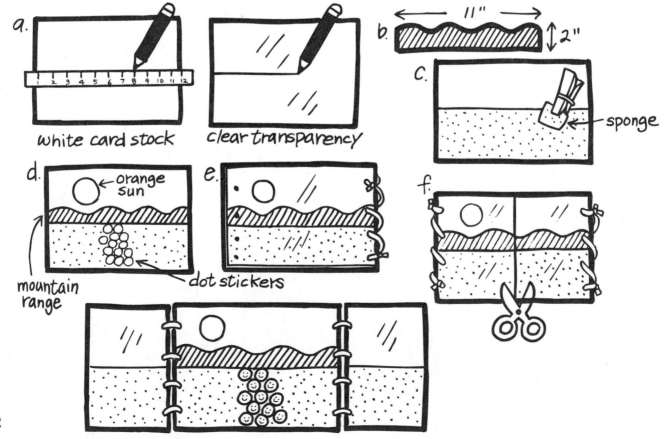

"Three Men in a Fire" Stick Puppets

(25-30 MINUTES)

Materials: Yellow card stock, red and orange food coloring, scrap fabric and felt, fine-tip felt pens, ruler, glue, transparent tape, pinking shears, newspaper, scissors. For each child—three tongue depressors, one plastic straw, six small wiggle eyes and three mini pom-poms.

Preparation: Cut scrap fabric and felt into 2-inch (5-cm) squares—three for each child. Cut card stock into 7-inch (17.5-cm) squares—one for every two children. Fold squares in half diagonally. Use pinking shears to cut square into two equal triangles (sketch a). Cover work area with newspaper.

Instruct each child in the following procedures:

❀ Teacher puts a drop of red and orange food coloring on bottom corner of card stock triangle. Child quickly blows through straw to spread the color (sketch b). Repeat if desired. Allow to dry.

❀ To make Shadrach, Meshach and Abednego, glue wiggle eyes onto each of the three tongue depressors (sketch c). Glue on pom-poms for noses.

❀ Wrap and glue fabric and felt squares around puppets to make clothes.

❀ Use felt pens to draw hair and other features on figures.

❀ With teacher's help, fold paper into a cone shape (sketch d). Tape edges closed.

❀ Place puppets in cone pocket to show Shadrach, Meshach and Abednego in the fiery furnace.

Simplification Idea: Draw eyes and nose instead of using wiggle eyes and pom-poms.

Enrichment Idea: Children cut tiny pieces of yarn and glue them onto puppets for hair and beards.

Pilot Briefing: **Shadrach, Meshach and Abednego loved God. They wanted to obey Him. How did they obey God?** (They only worshiped God. They wouldn't bow down to the king's statue.)

How did God save them from the fiery furnace? (He sent an angel in the fire to protect them.) **How can we show our love to God?** (Praying to Him, singing, going to Sunday School or VBS to learn about Him, being kind and loving to other people.)

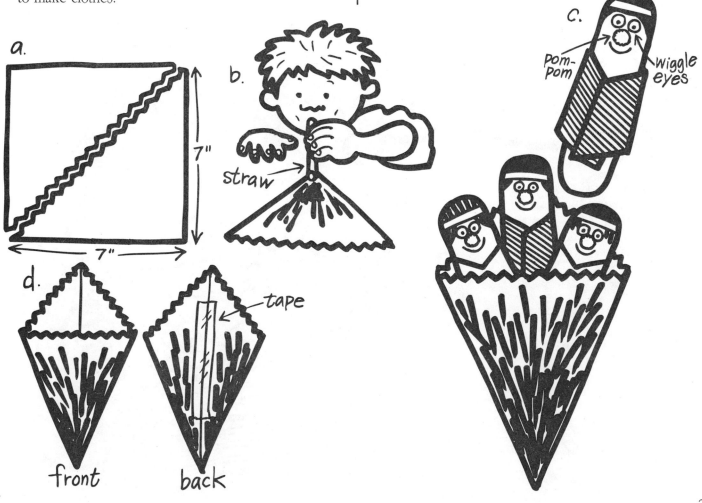

a.

7"

7"

b.

straw

c.

pom-pom

wiggle eyes

d.

tape

front

back

Jonah and the Big Fish Shaker

(10-15 MINUTES)

Materials: Jonah and Fish Patterns, white or blue plastic disposable plates, permanent felt pens, plastic fish-shaped confetti (found at craft or party supply stores), water, pitcher, blue and green food coloring, blue electrical tape, small fish or sea shell stickers, scissors, shallow containers. For each child—one small, clear plastic beverage bottle with cap.

Preparation: Trace patterns onto plastic plates and cut out—one Jonah and one fish figure for each child. Fill pitcher with water. Put confetti in shallow containers.

Instruct each child in the following procedures:

❀ Use permanent felt pens to decorate plastic fish and Jonah.

❀ Gently bend fish to fit through bottle opening and push fish into bottle. Put Jonah into bottle.

❀ Drop several confetti fish into bottle.

❀ With teacher's help, fill bottle with water until 1 inch (2.5 cm) from the top.

❀ Put a few drops of food coloring into water to make ocean. Use blue or green food coloring, or mix blue and green together.

❀ Put cap on bottle and twist tightly to close.

❀ With teacher's help, wrap tape around bottle cap to secure (sketch a).

❀ Shake bottle to mix food coloring with water.

❀ Put a few stickers on outside of bottle.

❀ Tip bottle back and forth to see Jonah and the fish swim under the sea.

Pilot Briefing: **What did God send to swallow Jonah and keep him safe in the ocean?** (A big fish.) **God loved Jonah and took care of him, even though Jonah ran away and didn't obey God. God loves you, too. He takes care of you by giving you mommies and daddies who love you.**

Fish Pattern

Jonah Pattern

a. wrap tape

"He Is Risen" Shadow Box

**(ONE- OR TWO-DAY CRAFT/
30-35 MINUTES TOTAL TIME)**

Materials: Angel Picture, photocopier, copier paper, ruler, lightweight cardboard, grey, brown and green tempera paint, fine aquarium gravel, course sand or bird grit, white glue, measuring cups and spoons, mixing bowl, paintbrushes, shallow containers, hole punch, yarn, ruler, paper clips, scissors, crayons, newspaper. For each child—two sturdy, large paper plates, one paper fastener.

DAY ONE

Preparation: Cut out center of plate slightly smaller than the size of Angel Picture (sketch a)—one plate for each child. Cut cardboard into circles or "stone" shapes the same size as Angel Picture—one for each child. With hole punch, punch one hole close to the edge of each cardboard shape. Make textured paint by mixing in bowl: 2 cups of grey paint, ½ cup of grit, sand or gravel and 4 tablespoons of white glue. Pour textured paint into shallow containers. Pour brown and green paint into shallow containers. Cover work area with newspaper.

Instruct each child in the following procedures:

❁ Paint the underside of cut plate brown for a cave and green for grass (sketch b).

❁ Paint one side of cardboard circle with grey textured paint. Let dry.

DAY TWO

Preparation: Photocopy Angel Picture onto paper—one for each child. Cut yarn into 6-inch (15-cm) lengths—one for each child.

Instruct each child in the following procedures:

❁ Use crayons to color Angel Picture.

❁ Cut out picture and glue to front center of uncut plate.

❁ With teacher's help, punch two holes in the cut-out paper plate as indicated in sketch c. Punch a hole at the top of uncut plate.

❁ Line up the holes at the top of paper plates and glue the rims of plates together. The Angel Picture will show through the cut-out paper plate. Have teacher paper clip edges until glue has dried (sketch c).

❁ With teacher's help, attach the painted "stone" to the top paper plate with a paper fastener (sketch d).

❁ Thread yarn through hole at top of plates and tie for a hanger.

❁ Cover the opening with the stone, then roll it away to see the angel tell the happy news that Jesus is risen!

Enrichment Ideas: Children may glue dried flowers and greenery onto grass portion of paper plate. Teacher may punch holes around the edges of paper plates and have children lace plates together with jute.

Pilot Briefing: **What did the angel tell Jesus' friends when they saw the empty tomb?** (Jesus is alive. He is risen.) **Jesus' friends were very happy. We can be happy that Jesus is alive, too. We can pray to Jesus anytime. We can talk to Him when we are afraid, sad or happy. Jesus loves and cares for us.**

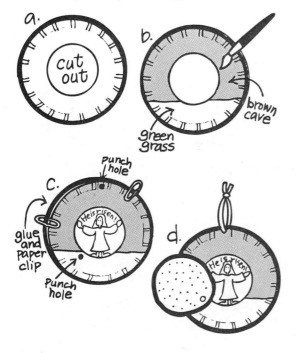

Angel Picture

House Napkin Holder

(20-25 MINUTES)

Materials: House Patterns, prepasted wallpaper scraps in a variety of small prints (include floral and foliage), pencil, scissors, ruler, craft knife, water, sponge brushes, shallow containers, damp sponges. For each child—one empty cereal box 2½ inches (6.25 cm) deep.

Preparation: Lay House Pattern on the corner of cereal box and trace outline. Repeat on opposite side of box. With craft knife or scissors, cut away box on lines to make napkin holder (sketch a). Cut out one napkin holder for each child. Trace door, roof and window patterns onto various wallpaper prints. Cut out two roof shapes, one door shape and four window shapes for each child. Cut wallpaper into 5x12½-inch (12.5x31.25-cm) rectangles—one for each child. Cut small bush shapes out of floral or foliage printed wallpaper—several for each child. Pour water into containers

Instruct each child in the following procedures:

❀ With sponge brush, brush the back of the large rectangle wallpaper piece with water to moisten wallpaper paste.

❀ With teacher's help, lay piece on the front of napkin holder and wrap around the side and back of the house (sketch b). Smooth wallpaper down. Wipe excess paste, if needed, with damp sponge.

❀ Brush water onto roof pieces and apply to house.

❀ Apply windows, doors and bushes to house in the same manner.

❀ Optional—Use felt, wrapping paper, construction paper or fabric instead of wallpaper.

Pilot Briefing: **You can use your house to hold paper napkins on your table at home. At mealtime you can help by passing out the napkins to your family. The Bible says, "With love, help each other."** (See Galatians 5:13.) **What else can you do to help at mealtime?**

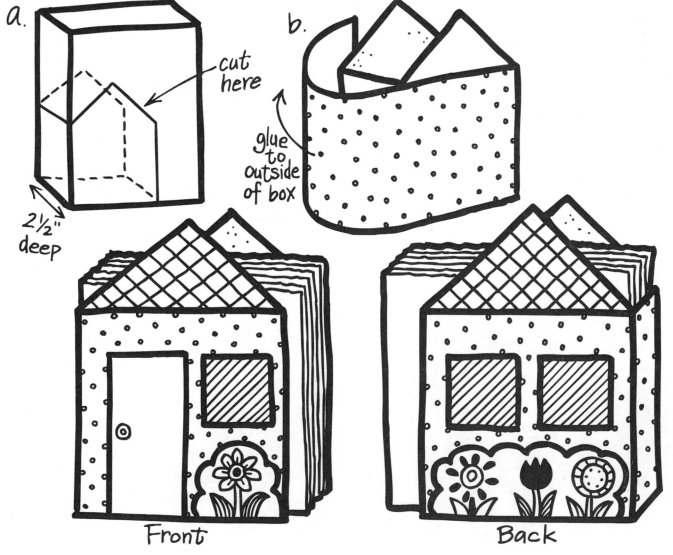

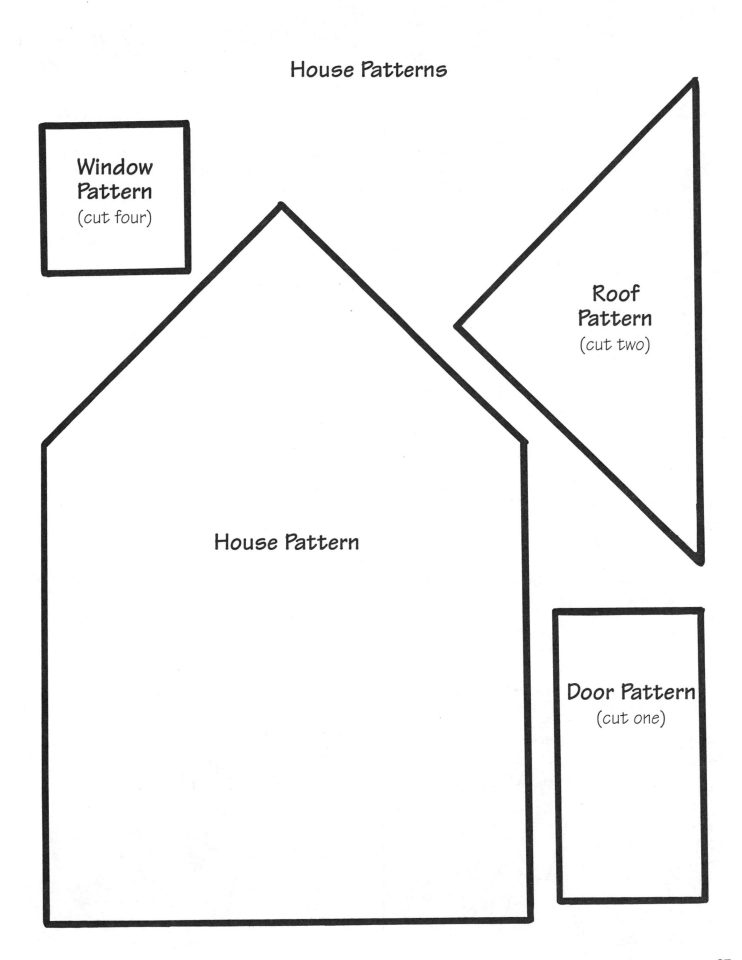

Window Pattern (cut four)

Roof Pattern (cut two)

House Pattern

Door Pattern (cut one)

Recipes 'n Memos Tile

(15-20 MINUTES)

Materials: Kitchen sponges, scissors, spring-type clothespins, glue gun, glue sticks, ruler, acrylic paints, unlined index cards, rubber stamps in hot air balloon shapes, ink pads, acrylic spray finish, shallow containers, newspaper. For each child—one white 3-inch (7.5-cm) ceramic tile, one spring-type wooden clothespin. Optional—permanent felt pens.

Preparation: Dampen sponges and cut into 2-inch (5-cm) squares. Clip clothespins to sponges to use as handles for sponge painting (sketch a). Pour paint into containers. Cover work area with newspaper.

Instruct each child in the following procedures:

❀ Dip sponge into paint and dab gently onto tile a few times.

❀ Repeat sponging with one or two different colors. Let dry.

❀ Using the rubber stamps and the ink pads, stamp a balloon image in the upper left corner of several index cards.

❀ With glue gun, teacher glues the wooden clothespin onto the center back of tile (sketch b). Tile will stand upright.

❀ In well-ventilated area, teacher sprays tile with acrylic spray finish.

❀ Place index cards in clothespin.

Enrichment Idea: With permanent felt pen, teacher letters "(Mom's, Dad's, Grandpa's) Memos" or "(Mom's, Dad's, Grandma's) Recipes" on tile before spraying with acrylic. Older children may letter a simple word such as "Mom" or "Memos" on the tile themselves.

Pilot Briefing: **Who are you making your tile for, (Shestin)?** (Child responds.) **Your (grandma) can use the tile to hold notes or recipes. Your tile will also remind her of how much you love her!**

Sharing Stones

(15-20 MINUTES)

Materials: Acrylic paints in various colors, shallow containers, large paintbrushes, thin paintbrushes, toothpicks, clear acrylic spray, newspaper. For each child—two smooth circular stones 3-4 inches (7.5-10 cm) in diameter.

Preparation: Pour paint into shallow containers. Cover work area with newspaper.

Instruct each child in the following procedures:

❀ Use large paintbrush to paint one stone a solid color. Set aside.

❀ Paint second stone a solid color. Set aside.

❀ Use thin paintbrush to paint hot air balloon designs on first stone. Make stripes with paintbrush. Use toothpicks to make small dots. Let dry.

❀ Paint designs on second stone. Let dry.

❀ In a well-ventilated area, teacher sprays stones with clear acrylic finish.

❀ Share one of your painted stones with someone you love!

Pilot Briefing: **You can share one of your painted stones with someone you love. Who will you give your stone to, (Abel)?** (Child responds.) **Giving gifts to our friends or family is one way to show that we love them. God loved us so much that He gave us Jesus. Who is Jesus?** (God's Son.)

Section Two/Grades 1–3

Crafts for Younger Elementary

Children in the first few years of school delight in completing craft projects. They have a handle on most of the basic skills needed, they are eager to participate and their taste in art has usually not yet surpassed their ability to produce. In other words, they generally like the things they make.

Since reading ability is not a factor in most craft projects, crafts can be a great leveler among a group. Some children excel here who may or may not be top achievers in other areas.

Many of the projects in the section for young children also will appeal to younger elementary children.

Pop-Up Balloon Card

(25-30 MINUTES)

Materials: Pop-Up Balloon Card Patterns, photocopier, yellow, white and brightly colored copier paper, pencils, 9x12-inch (22.5x30-cm) blue card stock, ruler, scissors, colored felt pens, glue sticks.

Preparation: Fold blue card stock in half to make cards—one for each child. Use pencil and ruler to mark a 2½-inch (6.25-cm) square in the upper right corner of back and front pages of cards (sketch a). Cut away squares. Photocopy Cloud Patterns onto white paper and Balloon Pattern onto colored paper—one set of photocopied patterns for each child.

Instruct each child in the following procedures:

❀ With pencil, draw a curved line diagonally from the top of the card to the corner of the square (sketch b). Cut on line.

❀ Cut out colored Balloon Pattern.

❀ Open card and glue paper balloon onto the curved section of card (sketch c).

❀ Fold card again with the inside facing out. Then fold the curved portion down diagonally. Turn card over and fold diagonally again (sketch d).

❀ Open card and fold in the original position. With teacher's help, fold the pop-up part of the card to the inside on the pre-folded lines (sketch e).

❀ Cut out a yellow circle for the sun. Glue to fold in the front of card (sketch f).

❀ Cut out large Cloud Patterns and glue onto front of card.

❀ With felt pens, write message on the clouds.

❀ Open card to the inside. Decorate balloon with felt pens and write message.

❀ Cut balloon basket out of yellow paper and glue in place.

❀ Cut out small Cloud Patterns. Write words on clouds for an additional message, if desired.

❀ Cut blue card stock into narrow strips, about 1 inch (2.5 cm) long. Fold strips accordion-style (sketch g).

❀ Glue one end of folded strips onto clouds, then glue opposite end to the inside of card (sketch g).

❀ Close your card, then open to see your message pop-up!

❀ Cards may be used in a variety of ways: Make VBS Closing Program invitations, get-well cards for hospital patients, encouragement cards for missionaries or thank-you cards for VBS directors and teachers.

Simplification Idea: Hand-letter card messages onto Balloon and Cloud Patterns before photocopying.

Pilot Briefing: **Your pop-up balloon card can show someone how much you love and care for him or her. When we tell people that we love or appreciate them, we are treating them the way Jesus would treat them. We can show Jesus' love to other people by doing and saying kind things to them. When has someone done something for you that was loving and kind?**

Pop-Up Balloon Card Patterns

Balloon Pattern

Cloud
Patterns

Hot Air Balloon Mobile

(30-35 MINUTES)

Materials: Balloon and Cloud Mobile Patterns (pp. 33, 34), Sun Pattern (p. 18), white poster board, old sponges, acrylic paint in a variety of colors (including light blue, yellow and orange), pencil, ruler, scissors, hole punch, string, newspaper, shallow containers. For each child— one wire or plastic clothes hanger.

Preparation: Trace Balloon and Sun Patterns onto poster board and cut out—one for each child. Trace Cloud Pattern onto poster board and cut out—two for each child. Cut a set of four lengths of string in various sizes from 3 inches to 12 inches (7.5 cm to 30 cm)— one set for each child. Cover work area with newspaper. Pour paint into shallow containers. Dampen sponges and cut into 2-inch (5-cm) squares.

Instruct each child in the following procedures:

❀ Use light blue paint to sponge paint one side of clouds. Let dry.

❀ Use yellow and orange paint to sponge paint one side of sun. Let dry.

❀ Use a variety of colors to sponge paint one side of hot air balloon. Let dry.

❀ When dry to touch, turn poster board pieces over and sponge paint the opposite sides of clouds, sun and hot air balloon in the same manner. Let dry.

❀ With hole punch, punch a hole at the top center of each poster board piece.

❀ Slip string through holes in poster board pieces and tie to hanger to secure, as shown in sketch.

❀ Hang your hot air balloon mobile in your room as a breezy decoration!

Pilot Briefing: If you were on a hot air balloon ride, would you like to fly above the clouds, in the clouds or below the clouds? What do you think you would see when you are in a cloud? When you are above the clouds? Some experienced balloon pilots say that flying inside the clouds and flying above the clouds is fun to do at first. But they enjoy flying *below* the clouds the most because then they can see how the land below them looks.

Cloud Mobile Pattern

Balloon
Mobile
Pattern

34

Sunset Silhouette

(25-30 MINUTES)

Materials: Sunset Silhouette Patterns, colored ink stamp pads in a variety of sunset colors (orange, pink, lavender, red, blue), pencil, old sponges, 9x12-inch (22.5x30-cm) white construction paper, 12x18-inch (30x45-cm) black construction paper, scissors, glue, transparent tape, black felt pens, newspaper.

Preparation: Trace patterns onto black construction paper and cut out—one for each child. Tape two sheets of white construction paper together—one set for each child (sketch a). Cut additional white construction paper into rectangle pieces to use for writing verses—one for each child. Dampen sponges and cut into 2-inch (5-cm) squares. Cover work area with newspaper.

Instruct each child in the following procedures:

❀ Tear off bottom fourth of top sheet of white construction paper (sketch b).

❀ Press sponge piece onto ink pad. Beginning at torn edge of paper, press sponge onto exposed paper and rub downward (sketch c). Fill exposed area with ink color.

❀ Tape torn paper back in place to cover painted area (sketch d).

❀ Tear off another piece of top paper about the same width (sketch e).

❀ Choose another color of ink and paint second exposed section using same method as above.

❀ Repeat procedure to paint a total of four different sections of paper with four different colors.

❀ Take off taped sections of paper.

❀ Glue hot air balloon and rider silhouettes onto painted paper.

❀ Letter Bible verse onto construction paper rectangle.

❀ Glue painting and verse onto black construction paper (see sketch).

Pilot Briefing: **The verse on your picture says, "Trust in the Lord and do good"** (Psalm 37:3). **When is it difficult to do good toward someone?** (Children respond.) **Your silhouette picture can remind you to ask God to help you (be kind to a friend who says mean things). You can trust God to help you do what is right.**

35

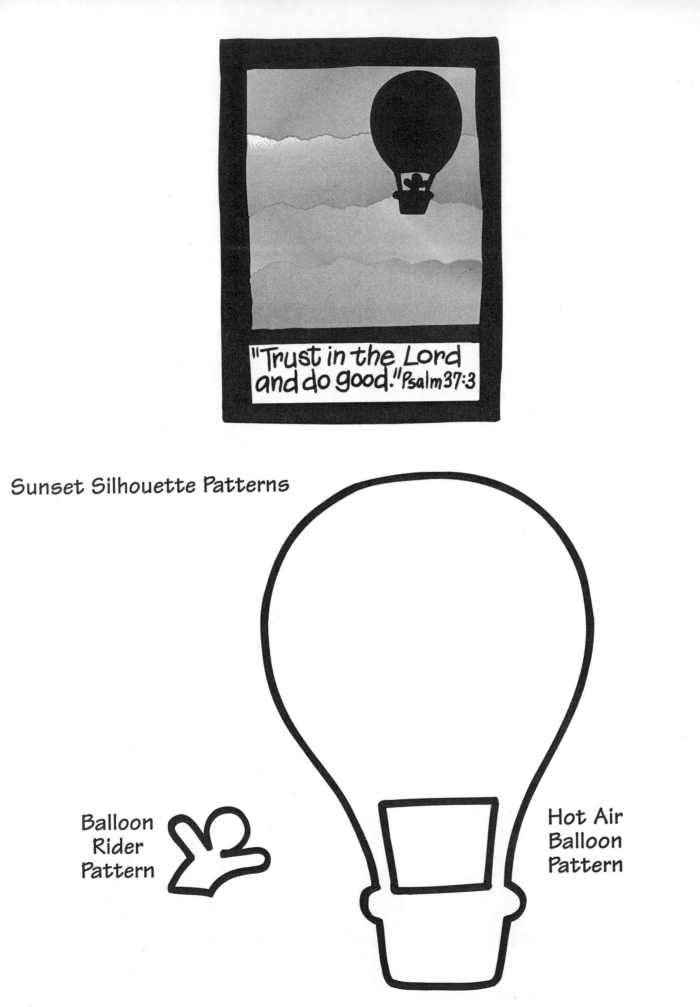

"Trust in the Lord and do good." Psalm 37:3

Sunset Silhouette Patterns

Balloon Rider Pattern

Hot Air Balloon Pattern

Hot Air Balloon Tote Bag

(25-30 MINUTES)

Materials: Tote Bag Patterns, fabric scraps, old buttons, fabric scissors, glue, thin black felt pens, pencils, tagboard. For each child—one solid-color gift bag with handle (found at craft or party stores).

Preparation: Trace patterns onto tagboard and cut out—one set of patterns for every four children.

Instruct each child in the following procedures:

❀ Trace patterns onto fabric scraps and cut out.

❀ Arrange fabric cut-outs on gift bag and glue in place (see sketch).

❀ With thin black felt pen, draw short dashes around shapes, outlining to look like stitching.

❀ Glue buttons on balloon, basket or mountains to decorate.

Enrichment Idea: Use your bag as a gift bag. Cut a long length of matching fabric and tie into a bow around the handle.

Pilot Briefing: You can use your tote bag to carry home the special papers and crafts you made at VBS. What have you done at VBS that you especially liked? (Children respond.) What's your favorite Bible story? (Children respond.) We each have our own favorites because God made everyone unique. That's what makes our world so interesting! And God loves each person just the way we are!

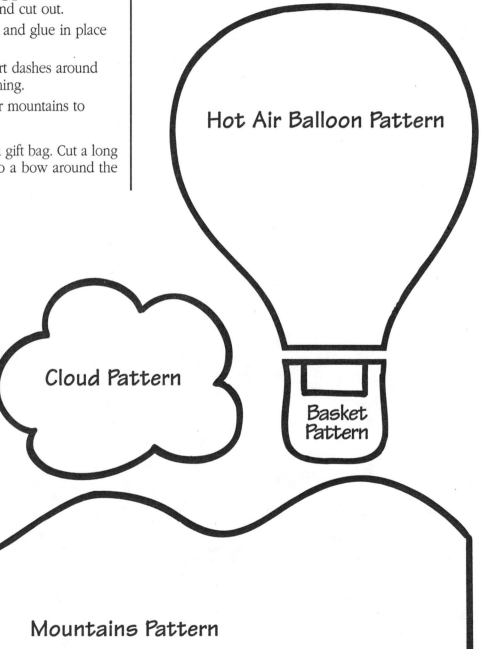

Hot Air Balloon Pattern

Cloud Pattern

Basket Pattern

Mountains Pattern

Adventure Kit

(30-35 MINUTES)

Materials: Old maps or map design wrapping paper, scissors, yarn, hole punch or awl, felt pens, glue, water, paintbrushes, shallow containers, sharp pencils. For each child—one box with lid (such as shoe boxes, laundry-detergent boxes, paper maché boxes purchased in craft stores, etc.), one small unlined index card. Optional—clear acrylic spray.

Preparation: Cut maps or wrapping paper into large pieces that are easy to handle. With hole punch or awl, make holes in opposite sides of boxes just below where the lid will lie (sketch a). Cut yarn into lengths suitable for box handle—three equal lengths for each child. Pour glue into shallow containers and dilute with a small amount of water.

Instruct each child in the following procedures:

* Tear map into various sized strips and pieces, no smaller than 2x2 inches (5x5 cm).
* Brush glue on outside of box and place map pieces over glue, overlapping pieces. Brush glue on edges of pieces to smooth down (sketch b).
* Continue in this manner, smoothing map pieces around corners and edges of box and lid. Cover top and sides of lid. Cover sides of box. Let dry.

* Find the holes on the box sides and use a sharp pencil to poke through the map-covered holes.
* Push three lengths of yarn through one hole and knot inside box (sketch c).
* Braid lengths of yarn.
* Push ends of yarn through opposite hole and knot inside box to form handle.
* Letter your name and "Adventure Kit" on index card and glue to box front or top of lid.
* Put lid on box.
* Optional—Teacher may spray boxes with clear acrylic spray before inserting yarn handle, to give Adventure Kits a more durable finish.

Simplification Idea: Use thick yarn or cording for handle instead of braided yarn.

Enrichment Idea: Letter Bible verses on additional index cards and place inside Adventure Kit.

Pilot Briefing: **You can use your Adventure Kit to hold items you would like to bring on your next adventure. If you could travel anywhere, where would you like to go? What would you bring on your trip?** (Children respond.) **Wherever you go, God is always with you. You can have faith that He will watch over and take care of you.**

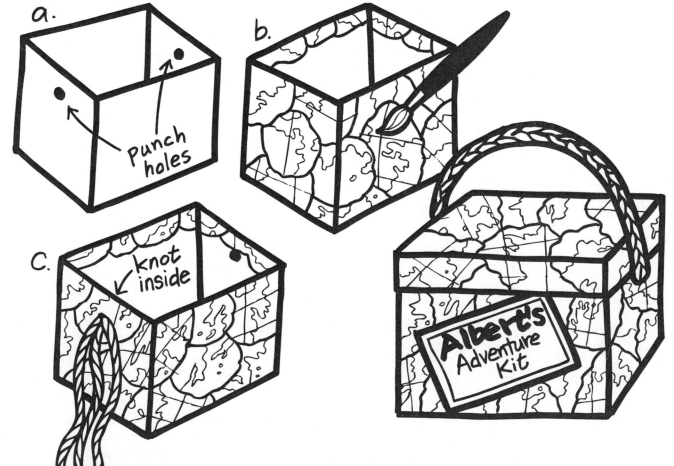

a. Punch holes

b.

c. knot inside

Albert's Adventure Kit

SonRise Balloon Gift Basket

(25-30 MINUTES)

Materials: ¾-inch gift wrap ribbon in a variety of bright colors, ¼-inch curling ribbon, measuring stick, scissors, transparent tape, permanent felt pens. For each child—one large balloon, one plastic berry basket, 5 chenille wires.

Preparation: Cut ¾-inch ribbon into 18-inch lengths—three or four lengths for each child.

Instruct each child in the following procedures:

❀ Starting from the inside of the basket, weave one length of ribbon around the berry basket until ends meet. Trim ribbon ends and tape together inside the basket (sketch a).

❀ Weave additional ribbons around basket in the same manner.

❀ Cut lengths of curling ribbon about 8 inches (20-cm) long and tie to corners on the top rim of the basket.

❀ With teacher's help, curl the ribbons with scissors (sketch b).

❀ Bend one chenille wire into a circle and secure by twisting ends together.

❀ Bend four remaining wires in half around the wire circle. Space the wires evenly around the circle (sketch c).

❀ Lightly twist each wire together.

❀ Attach each doubled-wire end around a corner rim of the basket, twisting wire ends to secure (sketch d).

❀ Inflate balloon and tie.

❀ Write a message or Bible verse on your balloon with permanent felt pens.

❀ Set balloon on top of chenille wire circle and tape in place.

❀ Fill the hot air balloon basket with candy or cookies and give to a friend or someone you love!

Pilot Briefing: **What are some things you could fill your balloon basket with, (Kendra)?** (Child responds.) **Who could you give your basket to? When you share what you have with others, you are doing what God wants you to do. You are serving God! The Bible says, "Serve the Lord with all your heart."** (See 1 Samuel 12:20.)

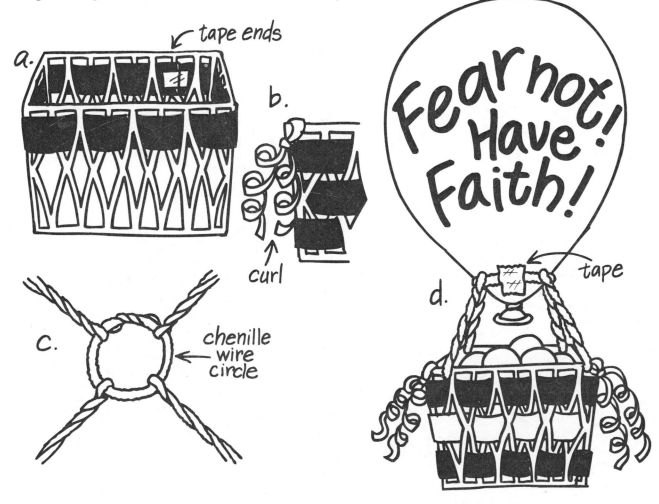

Alligator Puppet

(TWO-DAY CRAFT/20 MINUTES EACH DAY)

Materials: Green paint, cardboard egg cartons, stapler and staples, paintbrushes, shallow containers, newspaper, yellow construction paper, ruler, black felt pens, white poster board or card stock, scissors, glue. For each child—two paper fasteners, one empty food box (from crackers, cookies, croutons, cereal, etc.).

DAY ONE

Preparation: Cut off top flaps of each box (sketch a) and save cardboard flaps. Cut boxes in half lengthwise as shown (sketch b). Cut egg carton sections apart into two-section pieces. Pour paint into containers. Cover work area with newspaper.

Instruct each child in the following procedures:
* With teacher's help, staple a cardboard flap inside each box half, for hand grips (sketch c).
* Glue egg carton section to top of one box half (sketch d).
* Paint outside of box halves green. Let dry.

DAY TWO

Preparation: Cut white poster board into 1½-inch (3.75-cm) strips.

Instruct each child in the following procedures:
* Cut two white poster board strips to fit length of the box and two strips to fit the width.

* Cut a zig-zag pattern along one edge of all poster board strips to make teeth.
* Glue teeth to sides and front of box half that has egg carton section, teeth pointing down.
* Glue teeth to the front of the other box half, teeth pointing up (sketch e).
* Cut two semi-circles from white poster board for eyes. Draw two black circles inside each semi-circle. Glue eyes to front of green egg carton piece for eyes.
* Cut small rectangles from yellow construction paper and glue to top of alligator for scales.
* With teacher's help, join the two box halves together at back corners using paper fasteners (sketch e).
* Place thumb in bottom grip and other fingers in top grip to move alligator's mouth.

Pilot Briefing: **American alligators live in swamps, lakes and bayous. Is an alligator a mammal, fish or reptile? (Reptile.) Alligators are unusual reptiles because they care for their babies like a bird or mammal might care for its young. When baby alligators hatch from their eggs, the mother alligator cares for them and keeps them safe by carrying them in her huge mouth. How would *you* feel in the mouth of an alligator?**

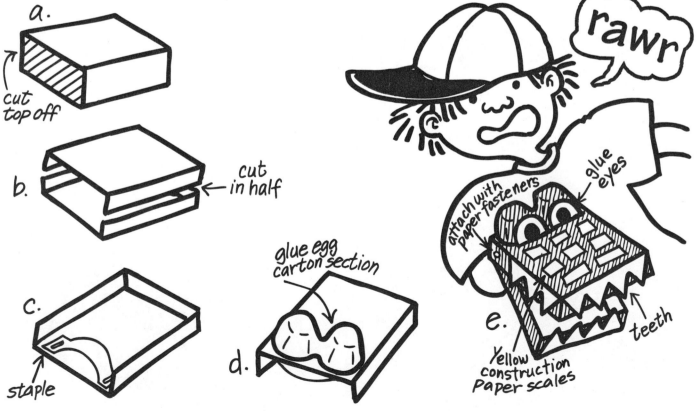

a. cut top off

b. cut in half

c. staple

d. glue egg carton section

e. attach with paper fasteners · glue eyes · teeth · Yellow construction paper scales

rawr

Dragonfly Magnet

(20-25 MINUTES)

Materials: Dragonfly Wing Pattern, tagboard, pencil, window screen, clear or iridescent glitter, acrylic paint in a variety of colors (including iridescent or pearlized colors), thin paintbrushes, craft glue, ½-inch (1.25-cm) wide magnet tape, pens, scissors, ruler, shallow containers, newspaper. For each child—two wooden spring-type clothespins, two small wiggle eyes.

Preparation: Trace Wing Pattern on tagboard and cut out to make several patterns. Cut window screen into 5-inch (12.5-cm) squares—one for each child. Cut magnet tape into ¾-inch (1.9-cm) strips—one for each child. Remove springs from only half the clothespins. Cover work area with newspaper. Pour paint into shallow containers.

Instruct each child in the following procedures:

❀ Paint two halves of separated wooden clothespin a solid color and allow to dry.

❀ Use paintbrush handle tip (not brush end) to decorate painted clothespins by dotting with contrasting paint.

❀ With a pen, trace pattern twice on screen (sketch a).

❀ Cut out two pairs of wings.

❀ Paint wings. While wet, sprinkle with glitter. Let dry.

❀ Lay one clothespin piece with flat side facing up. Center both pairs of wings and glue 1 inch (2.5 cm) from rounded end of clothespin (sketch b).

❀ Glue remaining clothespin piece on top of wings, flat side down. Use a second clothespin to hold together until dry.

❀ Glue magnet to bottom of body.

❀ Glue wiggle eyes on top of head (sketch c).

Pilot Briefings: **Where have you seen a dragonfly? (Students respond.) Dragonflies live close to quiet water. During the first part of their lives, they are called nymphs and live underwater in ponds and swamps. When the nymphs mature, they crawl out and attach to a reed. Inside the nymph's body, the dragonfly forms. When the nymph skin splits, a beautiful dragonfly emerges. Soon the dragonfly gracefully flies over the water and darts among the reeds.**

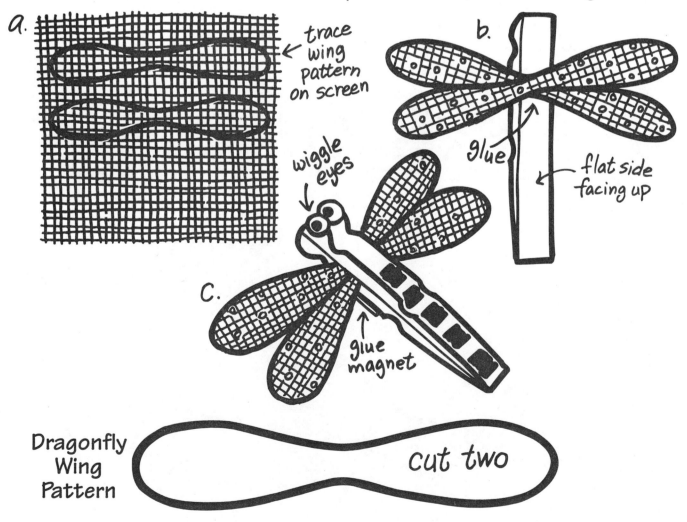

a. trace wing pattern on screen

b. glue / flat side facing up

c. wiggle eyes / glue magnet

Dragonfly Wing Pattern   cut two

Arctic Snow Shades

(10-15 MINUTES)

Materials: Poster board, cotton string, felt pens in a variety of colors, hole punch, paper hole reinforcements, ruler, pointed scissors.

Preparation: Cut poster board into 2x6-inch (5x15-cm) rectangles—one for each child. Cut string into 18-inch (45-cm) lengths—two for each child.

Instruct each child in the following procedures:

❀ Fold poster board in half (sketch a).

❀ Use scissors to cut off all four corners (sketch b).

❀ Starting at folded edge, cut a ⅛-inch (.3125-cm) slit in the middle of poster board. Stop 1 inch (2.5 cm) before the opposite edge (sketch c).

❀ Open poster board.

❀ Punch holes in opposite sides of rectangle. Place paper hole reinforcements over holes (sketch d).

❀ Use felt pens to decorate shades.

❀ Tie a piece of string through each hole.

❀ Tie the string around your head to wear your Arctic Snow Shades.

Pilot Briefing: **Eskimos used to wear goggles like these to protect their eyes from the cold, Arctic wind. A thin slit was cut to see through. The small opening also helped to dim the bright glare from the snow and sun. Eskimos carved their goggles out of whale bone or wood. They carved interesting shapes and designs on the goggles. How do you want to decorate your Arctic Snow Shades?**

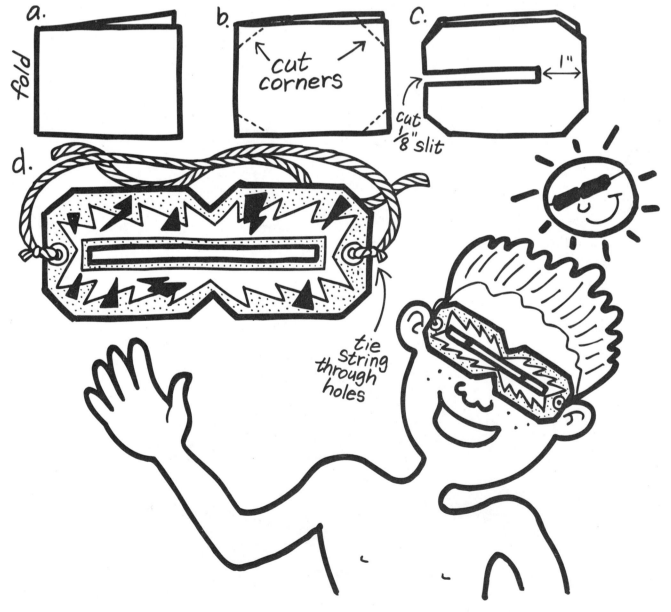

a. fold

b. cut corners

c. cut ⅛" slit 1"

d. tie string through holes

Plastic-Bag Parachute

(15-20 MINUTES)

Materials: Parachute Figure Pattern, white card stock, photocopier, colorful plastic shopping bags, ruler, yarn, felt pens in a variety of colors, scissors, hole punch, tape. For each child—one penny.

Preparation: Photocopy Parachute Figure Pattern onto card stock—one for each child. Cut plastic bags into 12x12-inch (30x30-cm) squares—one for each child. Cut yarn into 20-inch (50-cm) lengths—four for each child.

Instruct each child in the following procedures:

❁ Punch a hole in each of the four corners of plastic bag square (sketch a).

❁ Thread a length of yarn through each hole and tie to secure (sketch b).

❁ Gather the four loose ends of yarn together and tie at end (sketch c).

❁ Use pencil to trace figure pattern onto poster board piece. Draw and color figure with felt pens.

❁ Cut out figure and tape a penny to back side

❁ Use tape to secure figure to parachute where yarn is tied together (sketch d).

❁ Throw parachute in the air and watch it float to the ground!

Enrichment Idea: Use permanent felt pens to decorate plastic bags before assembling. Hand letter a Bible verse and child's name on bag.

Pilot Briefing: What keeps the parachute floating in the air, instead of falling straight down? (The air is trapped inside the plastic bag and pushes back.) **We can't see the air, but we know it is there because we see what it does. What other things do you believe in even though you can't see them?** (The sun behind the clouds, electricity, wind, God, Jesus.) **When we believe in something, even though we can't see it, we have faith in it. When we believe in Jesus and have faith in Him, we can become God's children.**

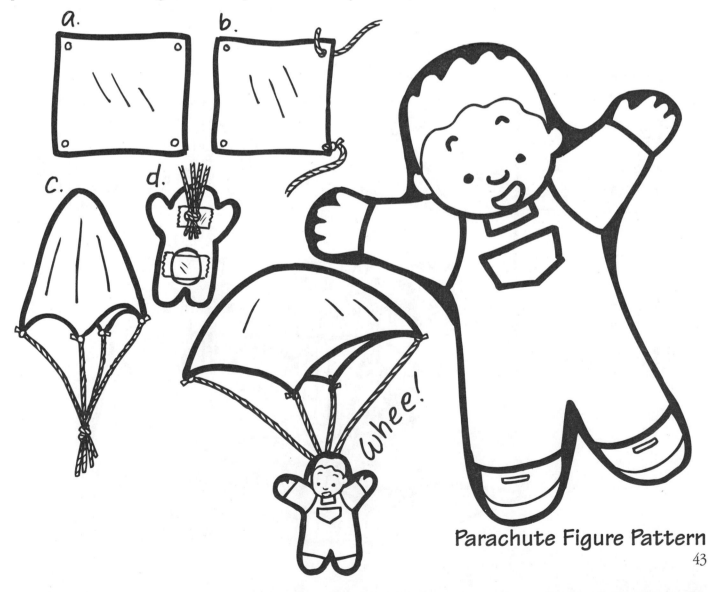

whee!

Parachute Figure Pattern

Stand-Up Picture Frame

(25-30 MINUTES)

Materials: Poster board, white corrugated cardboard (found at craft or school supply stores), pencil, colored felt pens, paper clips, ruler, scissors, craft knife, white glue, glue sticks, colored poster board scraps.

Preparation: Cut poster board into 9x22-inch (22.5x55-cm) rectangles—one for each child. Begin at one end and measure 4-inch (10-cm), 7-inch (17.5-cm), 7-inch (17.5-cm) and 4-inch (10-cm) sections (sketch a). Lightly score along these lines. Cut 7x9-inch (17.5x22.5-cm) rectangles from the corrugated cardboard—two for each child. Cut out a centered 3x5-inch (7.5x12.5-cm) opening from half of the corrugated pieces for photo frames (sketch c).

Instruct each child in the following procedures:

❀ Fold poster board piece on scored lines to make a triangle shape.

❀ Glue overlapping bottom sections together to make triangle board stand. Use paper clips to hold until glue has dried (sketch b).

❀ With felt pens, color each rib of corrugated pieces a different color to make stripes.

❀ Glue cutout corrugated piece to one side of triangle board. Glue only the side edges and bottom, leaving the top unglued so a photo can be inserted (sketch c).

❀ Glue second corrugated piece to the back of triangle board.

❀ Cut poster board scraps into triangles, squares, circles or other shapes.

❀ Using glue stick, glue poster board shapes around the photo frame.

Enrichment Idea: Take a horizontal photo of each child and develop ahead of time to insert into frame.

Pilot Briefing: Whose picture are you going to put in your frame? God takes care of us by giving us special people who love us. When you look at the picture in your frame, you can remember that (your dad) loves you and that God loves you, too!

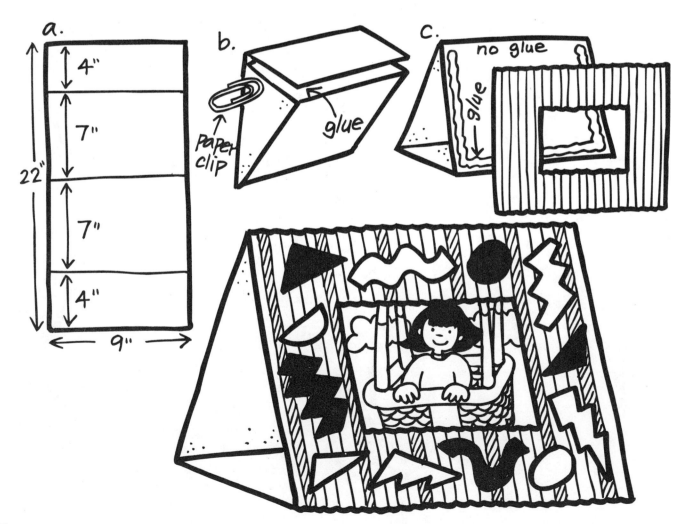

44

Stained-Glass Verse

(30-40 MINUTES)

Materials: White paper, pencils, wide and fine-tip black permanent felt pens, food coloring in blue, red, yellow and green, white glue, paintbrushes, poster board, scissors, ruler, hole punch, ribbon, tape, shallow containers, newspaper. For each child—one overhead transparency or one 8½x11-inch (21.5x27.5-cm) sheet of heavy clear plastic. Optional—one suction hook for each child, coloring pages (see pages 79-97).

Preparation: For the frame, cut poster board into 10½x1-inch (26.25x2.5-cm) and 13x1-inch (32.5x2.5-cm) strips—four strips of each length for each child. Pour glue into shallow containers. Mix food coloring in glue to make several colors of glue paint. Cover work area with newspaper.

Instruct each child in the following procedures:

❀ On paper, sketch a simple picture of a hot air balloon in the sky. Add a rainbow, clouds, landscape, etc.

❀ Tape transparency on top of sketch (sketch a).

❀ With wide-tip black felt pen, trace all lines of sketch onto transparency. Remove paper sketch.

❀ With fine-tip felt pen, letter "Trust in the Lord and do good. Commit your way to the Lord. Psalm 37:3,5" on bottom of picture. Allow 1-inch (2.5-cm) margin for frame.

❀ Glue four poster board strips around the edges of picture to make a frame on one side of transparency.

❀ Turn picture over and glue remaining poster board strips to the back, aligning edges with front pieces (sketch b). Trim pieces if necessary.

❀ Punch two holes in the top of the frame.

❀ Cut a 12-inch (30-cm) length of ribbon and thread through holes. Knot ends to make hanger (sketch c).

❀ Turn transparency over to backside and paint inside black outlines with colored glue. Allow to dry.

Enrichment Idea: Give each child a suction hook to hang picture in a window.

Simplification Ideas: Eliminate poster board frame and punch holes directly in transparency for hanging. Children trace photocopied coloring pages (see pages 79-97) instead of drawing pictures.

Pilot Briefing: **What do balloon pilots need to trust when they fly in hot air balloons?** (The weather, their equipment, their crew, their training, God.) **The Bible says that we can always put our trust in God. When we commit ourselves to doing the good things that God wants us to do, we can count on Him to help us follow through. We can trust God to help us do what's right.**

a. tape
paper with hot air balloon sketch
transparency

b. glue poster board

c. knot
"Trust in the Lord and do good. Commit your way to the Lord." Psalm 37:3,5

Jonah's Fishy Verse Game

(25-30 MINUTES)

Materials: Game Piece Patterns, construction paper in a variety of colors, photocopier, yarn, colorful fish or ocean theme stickers, glue, scissors, measuring stick, tape. For each child—one 12-inch (30-cm) stick or dowel, 12 small metal paper clips, one small round magnet, one plastic 2-liter bottle.

Preparation: Make copies of Game Piece Patterns on various colors of construction paper—four copies for each child. Cut the top off plastic bottles (sketch a)—one for each child. Cut yarn into 16-inch lengths—one for each child.

Instruct each child in the following procedures:

❀ Open paper clips as shown (sketch b).

❀ Cut out game pieces. Glue two identical game pieces together, placing opened paper clip between pieces (sketch c).

❀ Tie yarn around one end of stick. Tape magnet to opposite end of yarn.

❀ Decorate outside of plastic bottle with fish stickers.

❀ Place fish, Jonah and Big Fish game pieces into bottle.

❀ With one or two friends, take turns fishing. If you catch Jonah, you may use him for any part of the verse. If you catch the Big Fish, you may take a fish from any other player. The first player to place his or her fish in Bible verse order wins!

Pilot Briefing: **Who can say Galatians 5:6 in the correct order?** (Volunteers respond.) **Loving others is a way we show our faith. How would you show love or kindness while playing your fishing game?** (Take turns. Don't cheat. Be a good sport whether you win or lose.) **When you love God and have faith in Him, He will help you show love to other people, too.**

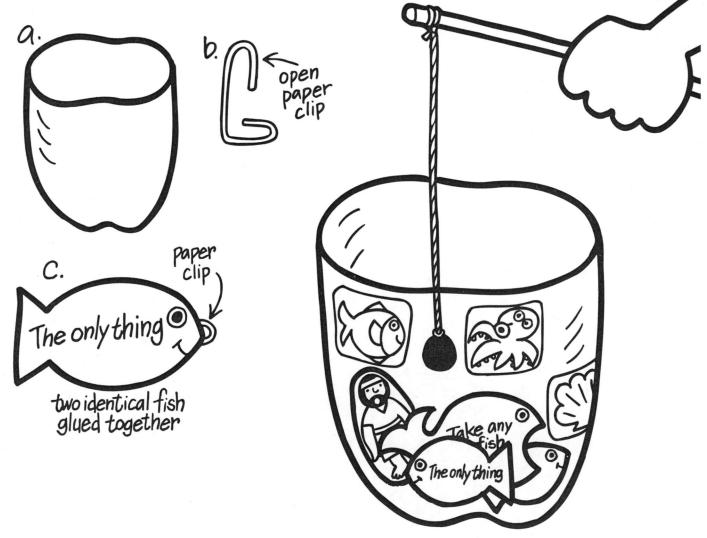

a.

b. open paper clip

C. The only thing

paper clip

two identical fish glued together

Take any fish

The only thing

46

that counts is

The only thing

Jonah
Wild Card

faith expressing

itself
through love!

Take any fish
from any player.

Big Fish

Galatians 5:6

(35-45 MINUTES)

Materials: Big Fish Pattern, poster board, blue or grey tempera paint, paintbrushes, black felt pens, pencils, ruler, fabric scraps, tissue paper scraps, construction paper, glue, glue gun and glue sticks, scissors, newspaper, shallow containers. For each child—one cookie, cracker or small cereal box, one wooden craft spoon, two small wiggle eyes.

Preparation: Enlarge Big Fish Pattern to cover boxes. Trace pattern onto poster board and cut out—one for each child. Cut out fin where indicated on pattern. Cut construction paper into 2x5-inch (5x12.5-cm) pieces—one for each child. Cut out an opening in the center of each box (sketch a). Pour paint into shallow containers. Cover area with newspaper. Plug in glue gun.

Instruct each child in the following procedures:

✤ Paint big fish blue or grey. Let dry.

✤ Imagine what Jonah saw inside the big fish. Inside opening of box, glue on tissue paper scraps to create a scene that looks like what Jonah saw (sketch a).

✤ With felt pens, draw hair, beard and facial features on wooden spoon to make Jonah figure. Glue on wiggle eyes (sketch b).

✤ Cut and glue fabric onto spoon for clothes.

✤ Use construction paper and cut out a conversation balloon. Write what Jonah might have said while inside the big fish (sketch c).

✤ With teacher's help, use glue gun to glue Jonah into the cutout opening of fish (sketch d).

✤ Glue the conversation balloon to look like Jonah is talking (sketch d).

✤ Use felt pen to draw eye and mouth onto big fish. Glue the painted fish onto box, with scene under fin.

✤ Fold back fin to see Jonah.

Pilot Briefing: **Jonah didn't want to tell the people in Nineveh God's message. So he ran away from God and ended up in the belly of a big fish! What do you think it was like inside the fish's belly?** (Children respond.) **What do you think Jonah thought while he was inside the fish?** (Read Jonah 2:1-3,7,9.)

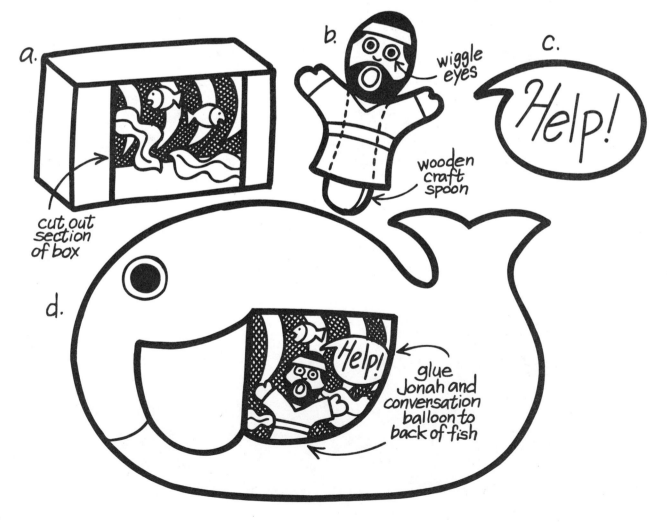

a. cut out section of box

b. wiggle eyes / wooden craft spoon

c. Help!

d. glue Jonah and conversation balloon to back of fish

Big Fish Pattern

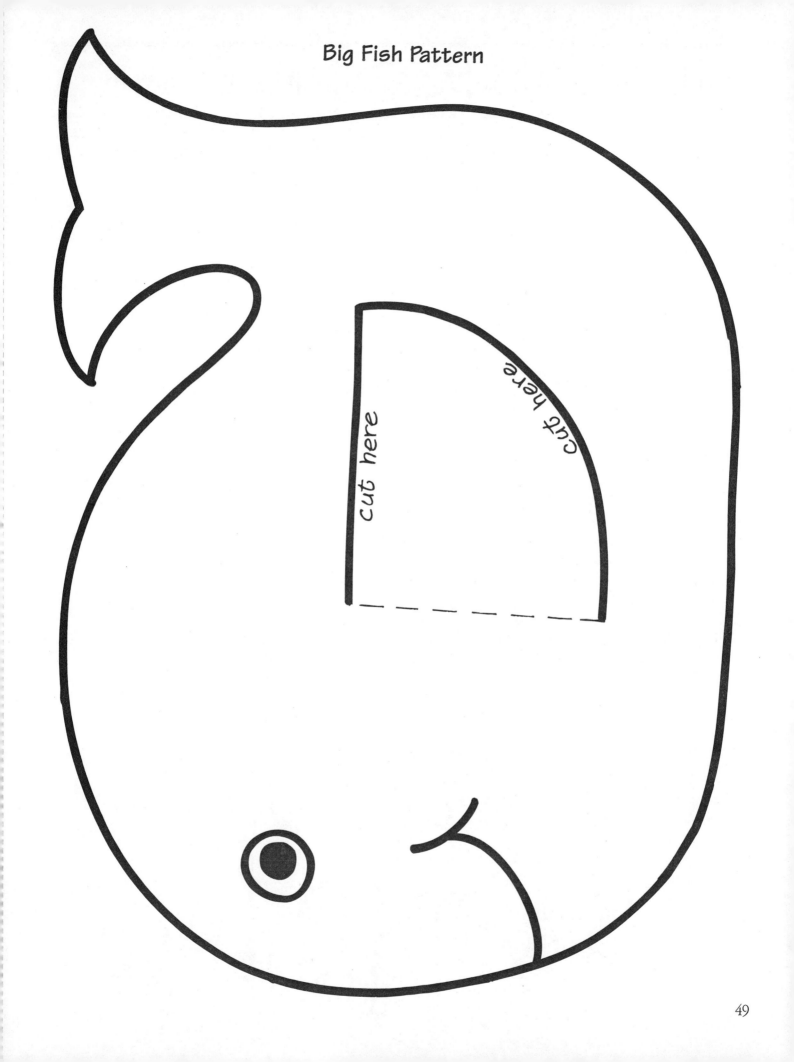

cut here

cut here

Shadrach, Meshach and Abednego Pop-Up

(40-45 MINUTES)

Materials: Yellow, red and orange construction paper, craft glue, small-sized rubber bands, scissors, thin black felt pens, ruler, fabric scraps. For each child—one half-gallon milk carton, one tongue depressor, four wooden craft spoons, six small wiggle eyes.

Preparation: Cut milk cartons to stand 4 inches (10 cm) high (sketch a). Cut a 1-inch (2.5-cm) slit in the bottom center of each milk carton. Cut construction paper into 5x12-inch (12.5x30-cm) rectangles—one of each color for each child. Cut fabric scraps into 2x3-inch (5x7.5-cm) rectangles—three for each child.

Instruct each child in the following procedures:

✸ Wrap and glue fabric scraps onto three wooden spoons for headpieces. Secure onto spoon with small rubber bands as headbands (sketch b).

✸ Glue two wiggle eyes onto each of the three wooden spoons.

✸ Use felt pens to draw nose and mouth on each spoon.

✸ Glue tongue depressor and wooden spoons together as shown (sketch c). Let dry.

✸ Cut construction paper rectangles into 5-inch (12.5-cm) flames approximately 1-inch (2.5-cm) wide (sketch d).

✸ Fold some flames (sketch e) and glue around top inside milk carton (sketch f).

✸ Glue six to eight flames around all four sides of milk carton (sketch g).

✸ Place tongue depressor through slot in bottom of milk carton. Shadrach, Meshach and Abednego are inside the fiery furnace! Say, as Nebuchadnezzar did, "Shadrach, Meshach and Abednego, servants of the Most High God, come out! Come here!" (Daniel 3:26) and move the tongue depressor up to make the men come out of the fire unharmed!

Enrichment Idea: Letter Daniel 3:26 on construction paper and glue to front of fiery furnace.

Pilot Briefing: **Why were Shadrach, Meshach and Abednego thrown into the fiery furnace?** (They would not bow down and worship King Nebuchadnezzar's statue.) **Shadrach, Meshach and Abednego knew that they should only worship the one true God. They loved God and wanted to obey Him, even if they faced danger!**

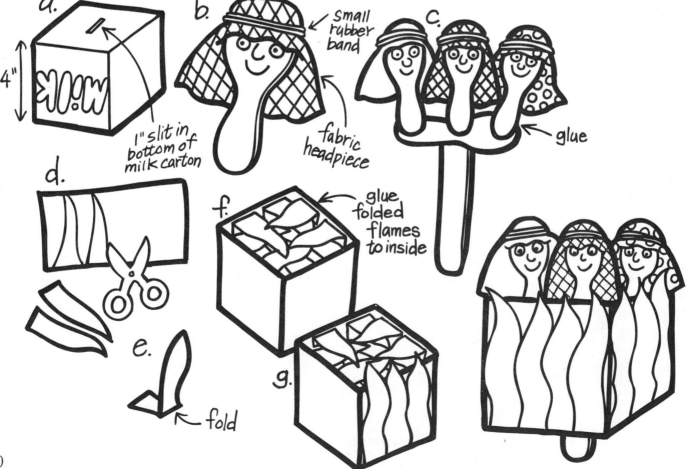

a.   4"   1" slit in bottom of milk carton

b.   small rubber band   fabric headpiece

c.   glue

d.

e.   fold

f.   glue folded flames to inside

g.

crafts for older Elementary

Trying to plan craft projects for older children has driven many teachers prematurely grey. The challenge is that while these children have well-developed skills to complete projects, they also have well-developed preferences about what they want to do. Thus a project that may challenge their abilities may be scorned because it somehow is not appealing to these young sophisticates. Then the next project will seem too juvenile to the adult, but will click with the kids!

There's no justice! And a sense of humor surely helps. One helpful device is to filter a craft idea through a panel of experts—two or three fifth graders. If they like it, chances are the rest of the group will, also. Then, the better you get to know your particular students, the better your batting average will be.

We think you'll find projects in this section to satisfy the varied tastes of older elementary children!

Balloon Gear Bag

(25-30 MINUTES)

Materials: Cloud-print or blue fabric, nylon parachute-type fabric in various bright colors, cotton or nylon cording, fusible webbing (such as Wonder Under), burlap, sewing machine, thread, straight pins, measuring stick, small bottles of fabric paint, scratch paper, pencils, iron and ironing board, scissors, masking tape.

Preparation: Cut fabric into 14x36-inch (35x90-cm) rectangles—one for each child. Cut cording into 40-inch (1-m) lengths—one for each child. Fold a ¾-inch (1.9-cm) hem on both ends of fabric and sew with sewing machine to make casing (sketch a). Fold fabric, right sides together and hemmed edges even. Sew sides of bag, starting from stitching line of hem and ending at the bottom of the bag. Casing openings should remain unstitched (sketch b). Trim corners and turn sewn bag right-side out. Make one bag for each child. Follow directions on package of fusible webbing and iron onto parachute material and burlap. Cut prepared parachute material into 3x7-inch (7.5x17.5-cm) rectangles—three different colors for each child. Cut prepared burlap into 2-inch (5-cm) squares—one for each child.

Instruct each child in the following procedures:

❁ On paper, draw an outline of a balloon. Make outline no larger than 7x8 inches (17.5x20 cm). Then draw a simple design on balloon (horizontal or vertical stripes, wavy sections, etc.) as shown in sketch c.

❁ Cut out balloon and cut apart on design lines to make pattern pieces.

❁ Lay pattern pieces onto parachute material and pin in place. Cut out patterns (sketch d).

❁ Peel paper backing from webbing on cutout shapes.

❁ Arrange shapes to make balloon on front of bag, fabric side up (sketch e). Fuse to bag with iron.

❁ Cut burlap piece into a basket shape and iron onto front of bag.

❁ Use fabric scraps to make additional tiny hot air balloons in the distance. Cut out and iron onto bag.

❁ Wrap masking tape around ends of cording to prevent fraying.

❁ Work cording through top hem of bag to make a drawstring for your Balloon Gear Bag.

❁ Use fabric paint to draw details such as *m* shapes for flying birds, dots or squiggles to decorate balloon, balloon ropes and your name (sketch e).

Simplification Idea: Buy inexpensive pre-made tote bags available at most craft stores.

Enrichment Idea: Embellish bags with buttons, ribbon or sequins. Glue on with fabric glue or fabric paint.

Pilot Briefing: **If you were going on a real balloon flight, what gear would you pack to feel confident and safe?** (Flight instruments, fuel, food, warm clothes, radio communication equipment.) **Being prepared often helps people have courage in new adventures. One way we can prepare to encounter new adventures is to pray and ask God to give us courage and confidence. We can have faith that God is with us. What new adventures and experiences have you had recently that needed confidence or courage?**

High-Flying Foto Frame

(TWO-DAY CRAFT/30-35 MINUTES EACH DAY)

Materials: Camera, film, heavy cardboard, toilet paper tubes, craft knife, ruler, scissors, hole punch, masking tape, pencils, shallow containers, white glue, water, aluminum foil, white acrylic spray paint, acrylic craft paint in blue, green, white, yellow and various other colors, paintbrushes, poster board or tagboard, ⅛-inch (.31-cm) satin ribbon, newspaper. For every two children—one 3-inch (7.5-cm) Styrofoam egg. Optional—clear acrylic spray, black medium-tip permanent felt pen.

DAY ONE

Preparation: Take a photo of each child standing up. Develop film same day. Cut cardboard into 6x8-inch (15x20-cm) rectangles—one for each child. Cut a scalloped edge at the top of each frame (sketch b). Punch hole in center top of each frame. Cut toilet paper tubes open and cut into 1½-inch (3.75-cm) sections—one section for each child (sketch a). Cut Styrofoam egg lengthwise in half. Mix equal parts of glue and water in shallow containers, making more as needed. Tear newspaper into strips 1 inch (2.5 cm) wide and 4 inches (10 cm) long. Cover the work area with newspaper.

Instruct each child in the following procedures:

❋ Fold ends of toilet paper tube section back to make 1-inch (2.5-cm) tabs. Tape to the center bottom of the frame to make balloon basket (sketch b).

❋ Stuff opening with newspaper strip.

❋ Glue Styrofoam egg half onto frame just below punched hole, with narrow end of egg pointing down. Tape to frame to hold in place.

❋ Dip strips of newspaper into glue, removing excess glue by pulling strips between fingers. Lay strips over Styrofoam egg and paper tube. Cover the entire front and back of frame, wrapping strips around edges and smoothing out wrinkles and bubbles. Cover with three layers of newspaper strips.

❋ With a pencil, poke a hole to uncover the punched hole. Smooth strips around hole, leaving hole open.

❋ Allow to dry on a length of foil that has been loosely gathered and formed into a circle (sketch c).

DAY TWO

Preparation: Spray all frames with white acrylic paint, front and back. Allow to dry. Pour acrylic paint into shallow containers. Cut ribbon into 10-inch (25-cm) lengths—four for each child. Cover work area with newspaper.

Instruct each child in the following procedures:

❋ Paint the sky blue.

❋ Paint the balloon and basket solid colors.

❋ Allow a few minutes to dry.

❋ Paint green hills, carefully painting around the basket.

❋ Paint designs on the balloon and the balloon basket (sketch d).

❋ Paint clouds and/or sun in the sky.

❋ Paint small house, if desired.

❋ Glue photo to tagboard. Carefully cut out your image, cutting off legs. Glue to frame, at the top of basket (sketch d).

❋ Glue four ribbons from the center top of the balloon to the basket rim, spacing them evenly (sketch d). Cut ribbons to fit if necessary.

Enrichment Idea: When paint is dry, students outline designs on frame with medium-tip permanent felt pen to give a "coloring book" look. Then finish with clear acrylic spray.

Pilot Briefing: Your frame can remind you that you are a special person to God. He loves you, just for being you. When you believe in Jesus and accept His love and forgiveness you become a part of God's family. He loves you so much, He sent His Son, Jesus, to die for you.

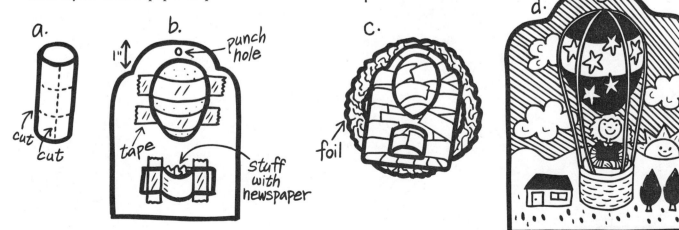

a.
cut
cut

b.
1"
punch hole
tape
stuff with newspaper

c.
foil

d.

Flying Fish

(TWO-DAY CRAFT/20-25 MINUTES EACH DAY)

Materials: Flying Fish Pattern, paper, lightweight clear vinyl (found at fabric stores), tape, permanent felt pens, measuring stick, scissors, squeeze-bottle fabric paints in a variety of colors including blue and green, paint shirts to protect clothing, straight pins, plastic lanyard lacing, several hole punches, iridescent cellophane or iridescent shredded gift filler, newspaper.

DAY ONE

Preparation: Use felt pens to trace fish pattern onto two sheets of paper. Draw dots from pattern onto fish. Cut out fish outlines and tape together at top (sketch a). Cut vinyl into 12x36-inch (30x90-cm) pieces—one for each child. Lay the taped double fish pattern under the vinyl piece near the top. With a permanent felt pen, trace the fish pattern onto the vinyl. Mark dots on the underside of fish that indicate where streamers begin. Use measuring stick and felt pen to draw a straight line from each dot to the end of vinyl piece (sketch a). Repeat process to make vinyl fish for each child. Cover work area with newspaper.

Instruct each child in the following procedures:

❀ Cut out vinyl piece, following marked lines. Do not cut top of fish apart.

❀ Lay vinyl on a flat surface.

❀ With felt pen, draw eyes and fins on top and bottom of fish, following example on Fish Pattern.

❀ Apply fabric paints to eyes and fins over the felt pen lines (sketch b).

❀ Decorate fish with fabric paint, using small repeated patterns such as wavy lines, small circles, dots, etc.

❀ On streamer section, paint blue and green squiggles to look like seaweed. Paint dots or circles to look like bubbles.

❀ Allow to dry flat overnight.

DAY TWO

Preparation: Cut lanyard lacing into 40-inch (1-m) lengths—one for each student.

Instruct each child in the following procedures:

❀ Fold double fish in half, matching edges to form one fish outline. Pin if necessary. Punch holes all around fish, spacing holes 1 inch (2.5 cm) apart and ¼ inch (.625 cm) from the edge.

❀ Beginning at the top of the fish, thread lacing through one hole. Leave 6 inches (15 cm) of lanyard extending from top of fish to use as a hanger.

❀ Continue lacing fish, but stop several inches before completing. Remove pins.

❀ Insert cellophane or filler to stuff fish.

❀ Finish lacing the fish closed. Lace ends of lanyard across each other and through two holes at the center top of fish (sketch c). Tie to make a hanging loop. Trim ends if necessary.

❀ Cut long vinyl piece into streamers approximately 1½ inches (3.75 cm) wide (sketch d).

Enrichment Idea: Have children draw and color a figure of Jonah. Then children cut out figure and place in fish before lacing.

Pilot Briefing: **The Bible says that Jonah was swallowed by a great fish, which might have been a whale. What do you think it would be like in the belly of a whale?** (Students respond.) **In 1891, a sailor working on a whaling ship fell into the sea. Three days later the sailors on the ship were cutting up a whale they caught. To their surprise they found their crewmate inside the whale's belly—alive!**

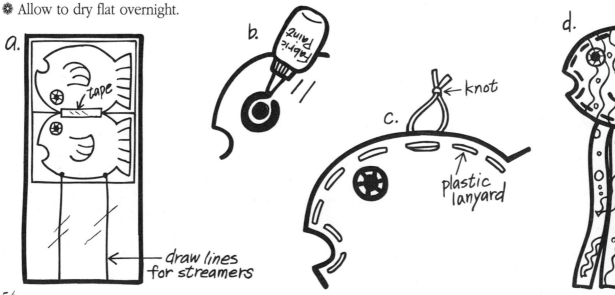

a.

b.

c. knot

plastic lanyard

draw lines for streamers

d.

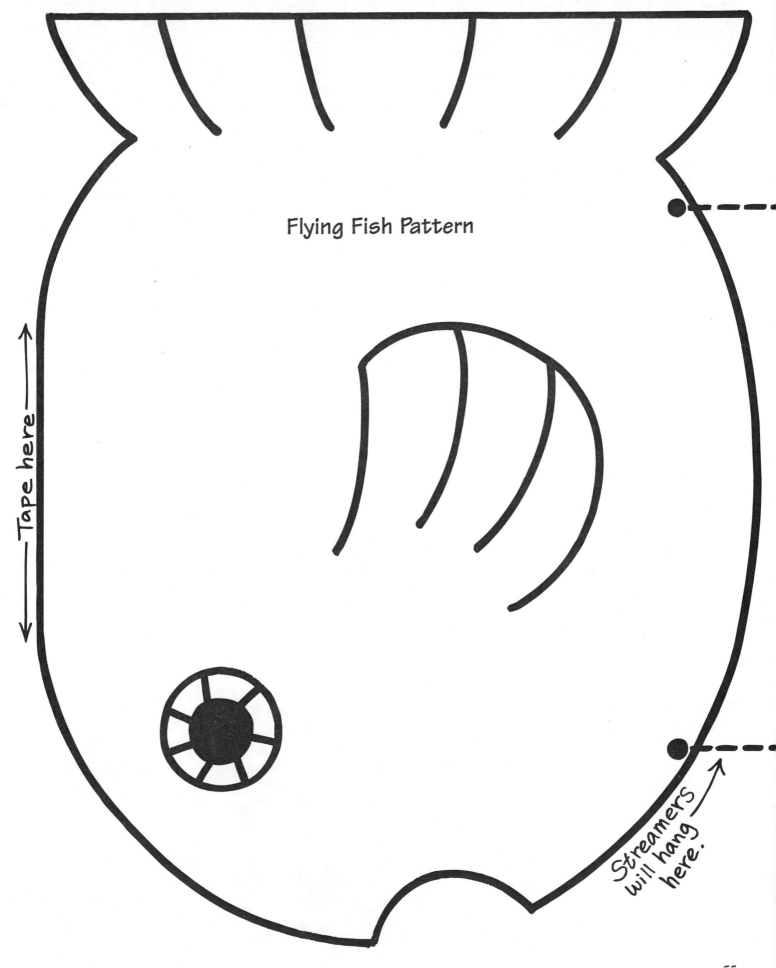

Flying Fish Pattern

← Tape here →

Streamers will hang here.

Balloon Banner

(ONE- OR TWO-DAY CRAFT/ 50-60 MINUTES TOTAL TIME)

Materials: White burlap, ¼-inch (.625-cm) wood dowels, saw, measuring stick, craft glue, assorted bright-colored felt or small print fabrics, fusible webbing (such as Wonder-Under), irons, old towels, pens, black crochet thread, straight pins, scissors, crewel needles, ⅛-inch (.31-cm) satin ribbon.

DAY ONE

Preparation: Cut burlap into 15x20-inch (37.5x50-cm) pieces—one for each child. Following directions included with fusible webbing, iron webbing to the back of felt pieces. Leave the paper backing on the felt.

Instruct each child in the following procedures:

❀ Remove enough burlap threads to allow for a 1-inch (2.5-cm) fringed border on all sides. Fold top 2 inches (5 cm) forward and pin (sketch a).

❀ Thread needle with black thread and knot. Stitch across top, ½ inch (1.25 cm) from folded edge, using a simple running stitch (sketch a). Knot and cut thread to complete.

❀ Draw shapes depicting the outdoors on the paper backing on the felt pieces. Be sure to include hot air balloon and basket shapes.

❀ Cut out felt shapes.

DAY TWO

Preparation: Cut dowels into 16-inch (40-cm) lengths—one for each child. Cut ribbon into 24-inch (.6-m) lengths—one for each child. Lay towels on a table for ironing. Plug in irons.

Instruct each child in the following procedures:

❀ Peel away paper backing from felt shapes. Pin in place on burlap banner.

❀ With teacher's help, iron felt pieces onto banner, following fusible webbing instructions.

❀ Cut three lengths of satin ribbon to reach from the mid-point of the balloon to the top half of the basket

❀ Knot ribbon ends and glue in place (sketch b).

❀ Slide dowel through casing at top of banner.

❀ Tie 24-inch (.6-m) length of ribbon to ends of the dowel for hanger. Add a drop of glue to secure knots at each end of dowel.

Enrichment Idea: Using crochet thread and needle, sew ¼ inch (.625 cm) overcast stitches along felt edges. Sew stitches unevenly and at different angles to look haphazard (sketch c).

Pilot Briefing: **When riding in a hot air balloon, first-time travelers are surprised to notice that they don't feel any wind. Why do you think they don't feel the wind?** (Students respond.) **Balloonists don't feel the wind because the balloon travels at the same speed as the wind. There is no air friction. Other vehicles of flight, such as hang gliders and airplanes often fly against the wind currents.**

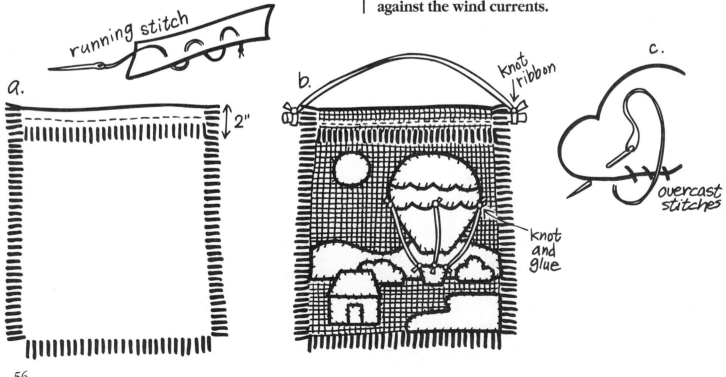

56

SonRise Balloon Plant Stick

(25-30 MINUTES)

Materials: Fabric in a variety of bright colors, fabric scissors, fabric stiffener, hole punch, glue, ruler, shallow containers, newspaper. For each child—one 3-inch (7.5-cm) Styrofoam egg or ball, one bamboo skewer, two chenille wires, one paper nut cup. Optional—Salt Dough (see p. 63).

Preparation: Pour fabric stiffener into shallow containers. Cut fabric into 1-inch (2.5-cm) squares, strips and triangles. Cover work area with newspaper.

Instruct each child in the following procedures:

❀ Dip one fabric piece into stiffener until saturated and smooth onto Styrofoam egg.

❀ Continue procedure, covering Styrofoam egg with fabric pieces.

❀ Punch four holes in nut cup (sketch a).

❀ With the pointed end of skewer, carefully poke a hole through the bottom of nut cup. Slide nut cup onto skewer.

❀ Glue skewer into narrow end of Styrofoam balloon (sketch a).

❀ Bend and glue two chenille wires onto balloon for ropes (sketch b).

❀ Poke chenille wire ends through nut cup holes and bend up wires. Adjust nut cup on skewer as needed (sketch b).

❀ Optional—Mold a Salt Dough (see p. 63) base around bottom of skewer to make balloon stand. Then set or glue balloon in SonRise Balloon Adventure 3-D Map (sketch c).

Pilot Briefing: **It takes some faith for a balloonist to launch his or her balloon. What are some things that a balloonist would need to have faith in before lift off?** (The weather, the equipment, his training, God's protection, etc.) **The balloonist has to have faith before he or she will have the courage to act. When we have faith in God, He will give us the courage to act and do what is right.**

Paper Maché Hot Air Balloon

(TWO-DAY CRAFT/25-30 MINUTES EACH DAY)

Materials: Newspaper, white glue, water, scissors, large paintbrushes, shallow containers, white acrylic spray paint, craft-weight tissue paper in various bright colors, pearl cotton floss, hole punch, ruler. For each child—one medium-sized balloon, one solid-colored paper cup, one yogurt container or small bowl. Optional—clear acrylic spray.

DAY ONE

Preparation: Tear newspaper vertically into 1-inch (2.5-cm) strips. Cut into 4-inch (10-cm) lengths. Inflate balloons to approximately 9 inches (22.5 cm) in length. In shallow containers, mix equal amounts of glue and water. Mix more as needed. Cover work area with newspaper.

Instruct each child in the following procedures:

❁ Set balloon in yogurt container or bowl to hold it upright while working.

❁ Immerse a single strip of newspaper in the glue and remove excess by pulling the strip between fingers. Apply strip to balloon. Smooth out wrinkles or bubbles.

❁ Cover entire balloon with two or three layers of newspaper strips.

❁ Set balloon on yogurt container to dry for 1 or 2 days (sketch a).

DAY TWO

Preparation: Paint balloons with white acrylic spray paint. Cut colored tissue paper into 1-inch (2.5-cm) squares. Trim paper cups to 2 inches (5 cm) tall. Cut pearl cotton floss into 16-inch (40-cm) lengths—seven strands for each child. Cover work area with newspaper.

Instruct each child in the following procedures:

❁ Cut a few large simple shapes (such as hearts, stars, moon, etc.) from tissue paper. Brush glue on balloon and glue on shapes. Then brush with more glue.

❁ Apply the tissue squares to the rest of the balloon surface in the same manner (sketch b). Allow to dry.

❁ With hole punch, make six evenly-spaced holes around rim of paper cup.

❁ Glue tissue paper shapes and squares onto cup to decorate balloon gondola (sketch c).

❁ Tie a strand of cotton floss through each of the holes in cup.

❁ Loop remaining length of floss with strands and tie the loose ends of all strands in a single overhand knot (sketch d).

❁ Slip balloon between strands of floss and glue knot securely to the top of the balloon, keeping the loop free from the balloon for hanging.

❁ Arrange the six gondola strands evenly around the balloon.

❁ Put a drop of glue where each floss strand rests on the balloon's midpoint (sketch e).

Enrichment Idea: Spray paper maché balloon with clear acrylic spray and allow to dry before assembling hot air balloon.

Pilot Briefing: **What is the balloon part of a hot air balloon called?** (The envelope.) **The ground crew lays out the envelope on the ground to get it ready for inflation. Then they turn on an inflator fan and fill the balloon with cold air. Only when it is nearly full, do they turn on the hot air burners. Then they finish filling the envelope with hot air and the balloon is ready to take off.**

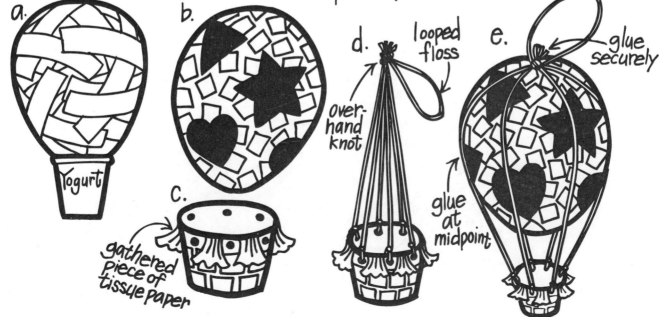

58

"Fear Not" Sign

**(ONE- OR TWO-DAY CRAFT/
50-60 MINUTES TOTAL TIME)**

Materials: Pine board, saw, measuring stick, hammers, acrylic paints in a variety of bright colors, glow-in-the-dark star stickers or paint, paintbrushes, craft glue, shallow containers, newspaper. For each child—one toothed picture hanger with nails, 16 2½-inch (6.25-cm) flat doll clothespins. Optional—small wiggle eyes, colored fake fur.

Preparation: Cut pine board into 4x15-inch (10x37.5-cm) rectangles—one for each child. Count 16 clothespins—one set for each child. For each child, cut six clothespins as shown in sketch a. (Remaining 10 clothespins for each child are used whole.) Cover work area with newspaper. Pour paint into shallow containers.

Instruct each child in the following procedures:

DAY ONE
❀ Nail picture hanger to the middle of the board with hammer.
❀ Paint the front and edges of the board a solid color. Let dry.
❀ Arrange clothespin pieces to spell "Fear Not" (sketch b). Do not glue in place.

❀ Paint clothespin pieces on all three sides. Use different colors so the letters are a variety of bright colors. Let dry.

DAY TWO
❀ Glue clothespins on board to spell "Fear Not."
❀ Glue glow-in-the-dark star stickers to the board or paint stars with glow-in-the-dark paint.

Enrichment Idea: Cut tiny pieces of fake fur. Glue fur and wiggle eyes to some letters as little creatures (sketch c).

Pilot Briefing: **What are some fears that people have?** (Students respond.) **Sometimes we are afraid of new situations or things because we aren't familiar with them. Sometimes we're afraid to do what's right because of what our friends might say. Some kids might be afraid to say no to an R-rated movie, or to be kind to an unpopular student. But once they learn that God will help them do what's right, they find it isn't so scary. What things have you been afraid to do in the past, but are more comfortable with now?** (Volunteers respond.) **Having faith that God is with us can help us "Fear Not" when we feel afraid.**

For each set cut:

6 top halves

1 double leg

7 single legs

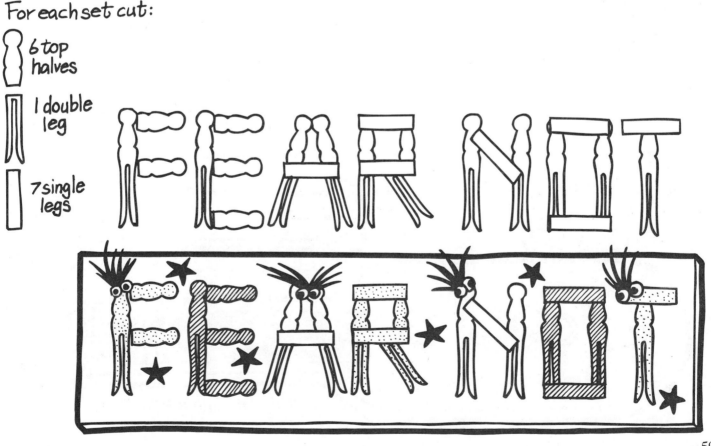

Kayak Paddle Plaque

(TWO-DAY CRAFT/20-25 MINUTES EACH DAY)

Materials: Paddle Pattern, lightweight cardboard, pencils, ruler, scissors, plywood, jigsaw or scroll saw, sandpaper, acrylic paints in various bright colors, paintbrushes, shallow containers, ¼-inch (.625-cm) auto-detailing tape in a variety of colors, drill, ⅛-inch (.3125-cm) drill bit, newspaper, hammers. For each child—two toothed picture hangers with nails, four screw-in cup hooks.

DAY ONE

Preparation: Trace Paddle Pattern onto cardboard, extending handle length where indicated (sketch a). Cut out. Trace pattern onto plywood. With saw, cut out paddle shape—one for each child. Drill four tiny starter holes on paddle for cup hooks (sketch c). Cover work area with newspaper. Pour paint into shallow containers.

Instruct each child in the following procedures:

❋ Nail one picture hanger near each end of paddle (sketch b).

❋ Sand paddle face and edges until smooth.

❋ Paint paddle and allow to dry.

DAY TWO

Preparation: Cut auto tape into 2-foot (60-cm) lengths—one for each child.

Instruct each child in the following procedures:

❋ With pencil, sketch the words "Be Strong" on the paddle handle.

❋ Cut auto-detailing tape into pieces to fit over sketched letters (sketch c).

❋ Remove adhesive backing from tape and stick in place on paddle.

❋ Add two bands of tape around end of handle (sketch c).

❋ Screw hooks into starter holes.

❋ Use your Kayak Paddle Plaque to hold your keys, camera or VBS crafts!

Simplification Idea: Children hand letter "BE STRONG" with paint or permanent marker.

Pilot Briefing: **Who can say the rest of this verse—Deuteronomy 31:6?** (Allow volunteers to quote verse.) **What are some things you do that make your body strong? Your mind strong?** (Students respond.) **What can we do that will make our faith strong?** (Pray, learn about God through His Word, learn from other people who know and trust Him.) **As our faith in God grows, He gives us more strength and courage, even when we feel afraid.**

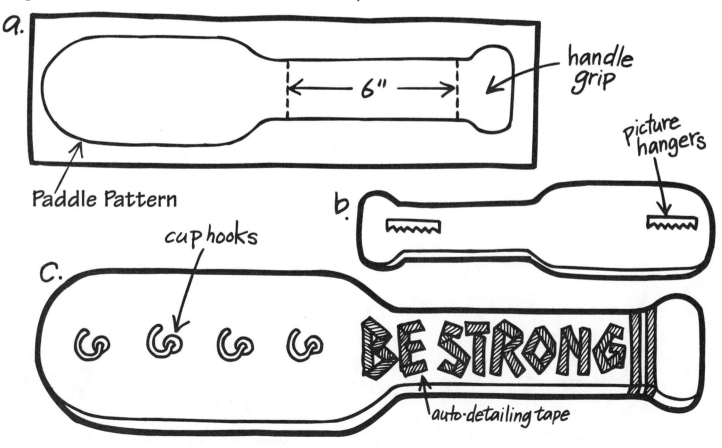

a. Paddle Pattern — 6" — handle grip

b. picture hangers

c. cup hooks — BE STRONG — auto-detailing tape

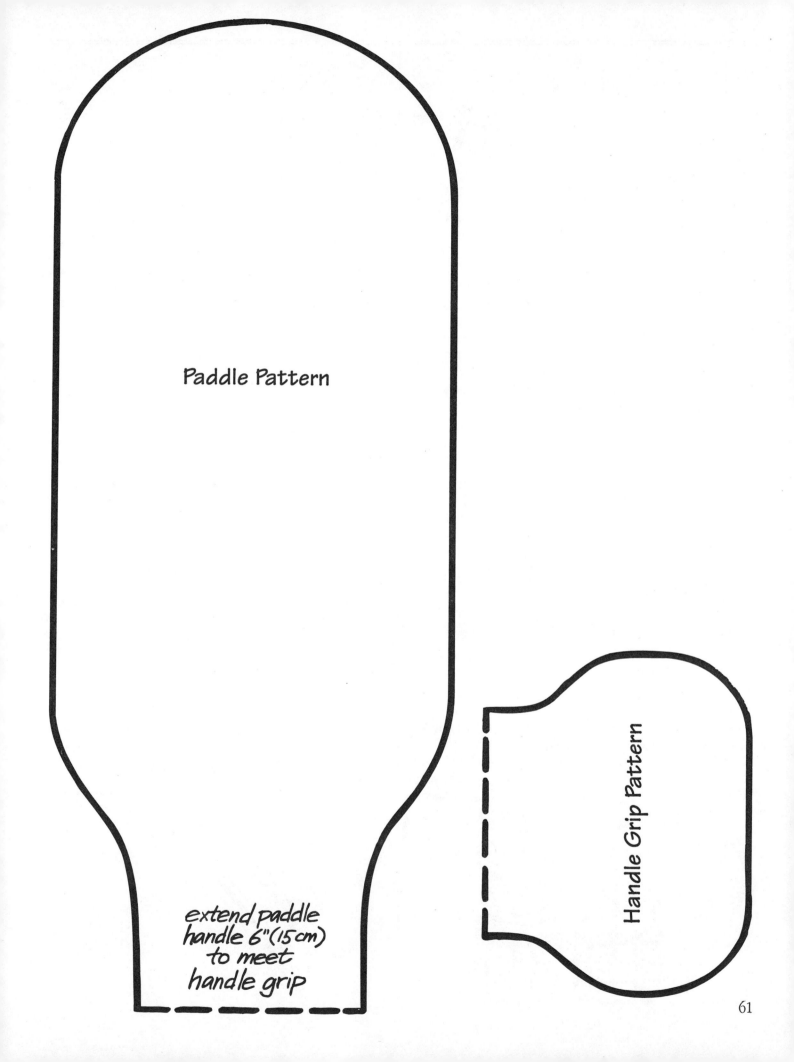

Paddle Pattern

extend paddle
handle 6"(15cm)
to meet
handle grip

Handle Grip Pattern

61

Fiery Furnace Candle

(20-25 MINUTES)

Materials: Table salt, candle wicks, scissors, ruler, black, red, orange and yellow dry tempera paint, paraffin wax, measuring utensils, spoons, bamboo skewers, four shallow containers, empty coffee can, stove, saucepan, water. For each child—one clean baby food jar.

Preparation: Cut candle wick into 3-inch (7.5-cm) lengths. Pour 1 cup (.24 l) of salt into each container. Mix 1 tsp. dry tempera into each container of salt to make four colors. (Add more tempera for greater color intensity.) Melt wax in a can set into a saucepan of water. Heat on low. (Watch closely as wax will melt quickly.)

Instruct each child in the following procedures:

❀ Spoon defined layers of red, orange and yellow salt into the jar.

❀ Add a final layer of black salt, stopping 1 inch (2.5 cm) from top of jar (sketch a).

❀ Press a skewer against the inside of the jar and push skewer down through all salt layers. Carefully pull skewer out and repeat procedure around the sides of the jar to make "flames" (sketch b).

❀ Push the wick down through the middle of the salt (sketch c).

❀ With adult supervision, carefully pour the hot wax into the jar, filling it to the top (sketch c).

❀ Trim wick if necessary.

❀ Allow wax to harden.

Pilot Briefing: **What is a furnace?** (Students respond. They may mention fireplaces or furnaces that heat their houses.) **In the Bible, the fiery furnace that Shadrach, Meshach and Abednego were thrown into was probably used as a huge kiln to fire pottery. Even though they faced death in the fire, Shadrach, Meshach and Abednego showed their faith in God by obeying Him.**

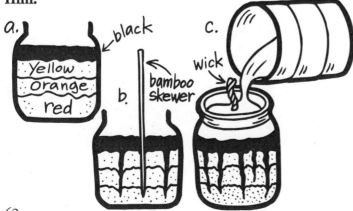

Moses Key Ring

(20-25 MINUTES)

Materials: Acrylic paints in peach, brown, blue and grey, small paintbrushes, black fine-tip permanent felt pen, drill, ⅛-inch (.3125-cm) drill bit, shallow containers, newspaper. For each child—one large wooden, flat doll clothespin, one eye hook, one split key ring.

Preparation: Drill starter hole in top of each clothespin. Cover work area with newspaper. Pour acrylic paint into shallow containers.

Instruct each child in the following procedures:

❀ Paint lower portion of clothespin brown for body. Paint peach skin-tone face, grey hair and beard and blue headdress. (See sketch.) Let dry.

❀ Add facial features and headband with felt pen.

❀ Screw eye hook into top of head.

❀ Attach key ring.

Enrichment Idea: Children make other Bible people of faith (Elisha, Jonah, Shadrach, Meshach, Abednego, etc.). Hang several Bible characters together to make a mobile.

Pilot Briefing: **When Moses and the Israelites came to the Red Sea, what did God tell Moses to do?** (Hold up his staff.) **Moses had faith that God would help them escape from the Egyptians. But he also did his part by listening to God. We can have faith that God is with us, too. God also wants *us* to listen to Him and follow His instructions every day. How can we listen to God?** (Read the Bible, learn about Him at VBS or church, pray, etc.)

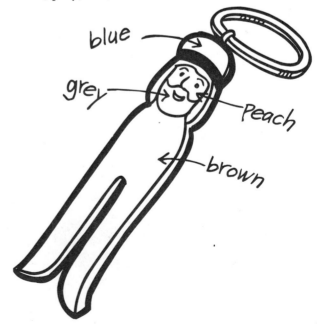

Group Project

(THREE-DAY CRAFT/30 MINUTES EACH DAY)

In this project, each child creates a 3-D map of one of the five regions visited in the *SonRise Balloon Adventure*—canyon, swamp, volcano, ocean and Arctic (see detailed instructions on pp. 64-68). When the maps are completed, the children display the maps together to make one large 3-D map which is viewed by friends, parents and relatives at the Closing Program. After VBS, each child may take home his or her part of the map.

Enrichment Ideas: Set up a 3-D Map Center so children may work on their map throughout the week of VBS, adding as many details as they can dream up. The SonRise Balloon Plant Stick craft (see p. 57) may also be added to each child's map.

Simplification Ideas: Choose only one region for an entire class to make. On Day Three, use paint for details instead of the Soap Dough.

DAY ONE—FORM THE MAP WITH SALT DOUGH

Materials: Mat board or heavy cardboard, ruler, pencil, craft knife, flour, salt, water, measuring cup, large mixing bowl, wooden spoon, photocopier, copier paper, Map Region instruction sketches, aluminum foil, toothpicks, newspaper. *For Swamp*—green food coloring, 10-20 forked twigs for each child. *For Volcano*—smooth twigs. *For Arctic*—permanent felt pens, scissors, sugar cubes, glue, rubber cement, one blank overhead transparency for every two children. Optional—magazine pictures of each region.

Preparation: With craft knife, cut cardboard into 1-foot (30-cm) squares—one for each child. Photocopy several copies of each Map Region sketch (on following pages) for children to refer to. To make Salt Dough, use wooden spoon to mix 8 cups flour, 8 cups salt, and 6 cups water together in large bowl—one batch of dough for every four children. Dough should be slightly sticky. Add more flour to a small portion of dough to make the dough pliable for modeling small figures. (Note: Salt Dough may be made the day before craft, if kept in air-tight containers.) Cover work area with newspaper. *For Swamp*—mix green food coloring into Salt Dough. *For Volcano*—cut smooth twigs into 2-inch (5-cm) pieces. *For Arctic*—cut transparencies in half—one half for each child.

DAY TWO—PAINT AND/OR ADD TREES

Materials: Tempera paints in red, orange, brown, blue, black, grey, white, pink and green, paintbrushes, shallow containers, glue, newspaper. *For Swamp*—Spanish moss, white glow-in-the-dark fine-tip fabric paint. *For Ocean*—sand, plastic cup, large shallow box.

Preparation: Pour paints into shallow containers. Cover work area with newspaper. *For Canyon*—mix red and orange paint together to make a reddish-orange color. *For Ocean*—pour glue into a shallow container. *For Arctic*—mix a small amount of blue and pink paint with white paint to make very light pink and blue colors.

DAY THREE—ADD SOAP DOUGH AND MINIATURE DETAILS

Materials: Soap powder (such as Ivory Snow), warm water, measuring cup, large bowl, electric mixer, plastic knives, spoons, scissors, construction paper in various colors including yellow, brown, green and orange, fine-tip felt pens, glue, blue plastic wrap, shallow containers. *For Canyon*—Spanish moss (available in craft stores), sand, red aquarium gravel, yellow yarn. *For Swamp*—green food coloring, pine needles. *For Volcano*—red food coloring, black aquarium gravel, red and orange cellophane, green tissue paper, transparent tape. *For Ocean*—toothpicks, small twigs. *For Arctic*—iridescent glitter, white Styrofoam broken into small chunks.

Preparation: Pour sand and gravel into containers. To make Soap Dough, pour 2 cups soap powder and 1 cup warm water in large bowl. Beat with mixer until thick. (Note: Make dough same day as craft.) *For Canyon and Ocean*—make one recipe for every 15 children. *For Swamp*—make one recipe for every three children. Mix green food coloring into soap dough. *For Volcano*—make one recipe for every five children. Mix red food coloring into Soap Dough. *For Arctic*—make one recipe for every three children.

Canyon Region (3-D Map)

(For materials and preparation see p. 63.)

LANDSCAPE FEATURES:
Tall, sheer canyon walls with a river gorge, trails along edge of cliffs, waterfalls, rock formations.

DAY ONE
Instruct each child in the following procedures:
❋ Spread a thin layer of Salt Dough onto cardboard base.
❋ Crush foil to form cliffs (sketch a). Place on base and spread Salt Dough over foil
❋ Use Salt Dough to form mountains, rock formations, trails and river gorge (sketch b).
❋ Allow to dry overnight.

DAY TWO
Instruct each child in the following procedures:
❋ Paint cliffs and trails red-orange.
❋ Paint waterfalls blue.
❋ Paint rock formations reddish-brown
❋ Allow paint to dry overnight

DAY THREE
Instruct each child in the following procedures:
❋ With plastic knife, spread glue on river gorge. Use spoon to sprinkle sand over glue for a sandy riverbed (sketch c).
❋ Glue red gravel along river banks.
❋ Tear off a long piece of blue plastic wrap. Bunch up width of plastic wrap and glue onto sand to make the river (sketch c).
❋ Cut a small oval out of yellow construction paper. Glue a length of yellow yarn along edge of oval to make a river raft (sketch d). Glue onto river.
❋ Glue moss along edges of trails as foliage.
❋ With knife, dab Soap Dough at base of waterfall to create foam and dot on the river to make rapids.

Pilot Briefing: **Have you ever gone river rafting or kayaking? Experienced "river rats" (as rafters are sometimes called) say that rafters need more skill than strength. Knowing they have learned the right techniques gives them courage when they face challenging river rapids. Sometimes we face challenges and we need courage, too. Getting to know God through prayer and learning about Him in the Bible will help us have courage in challenging situations.**

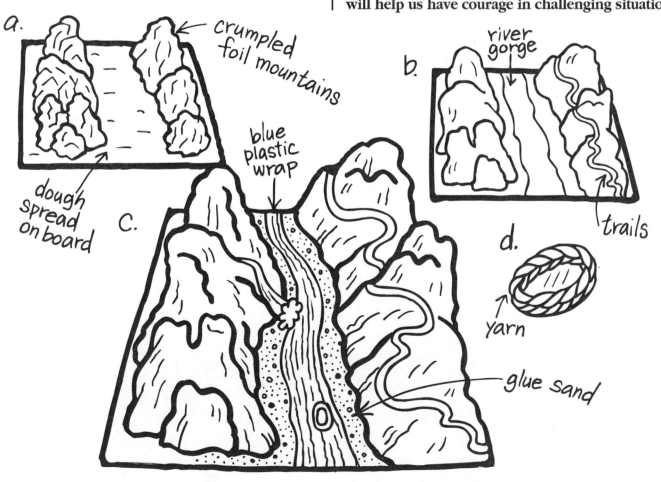

a. crumpled foil mountains

dough spread on board

c. blue plastic wrap

b. river gorge

trails

d. yarn

glue sand

Swamp Region (3-D Map)

(For materials and preparation see p. 63.)

LANDSCAPE FEATURES:
Flat land with dense trees and many waterways.

DAY ONE
Instruct each child in the following procedures:
❁ Spread Salt Dough onto cardboard base. Make shallow indentations for waterways (sketch a).
❁ Stick twigs into dough to make trees.
❁ Allow to dry overnight.

DAY TWO
Instruct each child in the following procedures:
❁ Glue thick patches of Spanish moss around waterways.
❁ Glue moss on twigs for trees (sketch b).
❁ Dot fabric paint on trees for fireflies.

DAY THREE
Instruct each child in the following procedures:
❁ With a spoon, spread a smooth layer of green Soap Dough in swamp waterways (sketch c).
❁ Cut a small rectangular piece of brown construction paper. Fold in half lengthwise and cut off corners (sketch d).
❁ Glue sides of paper to make a canoe. Place canoe in swamp water.
❁ Cut pine needles in half.
❁ Insert several pine needles into swamp water for reeds.

Pilot Briefing: **If you flew a hot air balloon over a swamp, your balloon would probably lose altitude. The moisture in the air over swampy areas tends to pull a balloon lower. How do you think dry, open areas affect a balloon?** (Make it rise higher.) **Sometimes *people* can feel "up" or "down." What things can bring you down? What lifts you up?** (Students respond.) **God wants us to lift up each other. What could you do to lift up someone who is feeling down?**

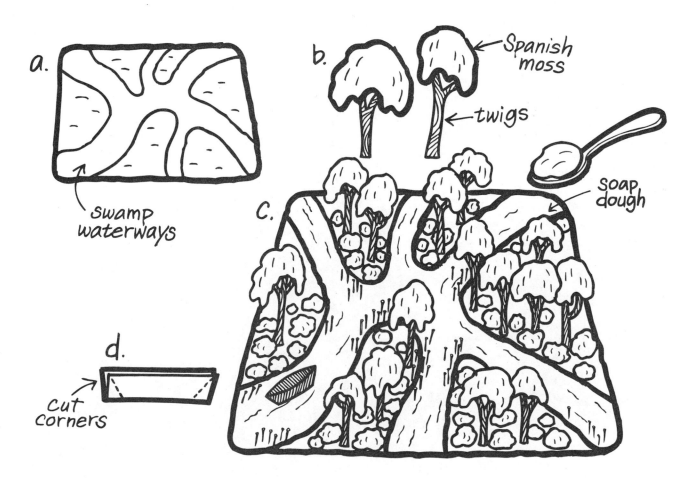

a. swamp waterways

b. Spanish moss — twigs

c. soap dough

d. cut corners

65

Volcano Region (3-D Map)

(For materials and preparation see p. 63.)

LANDSCAPE FEATURES:
Large volcano surrounded by flat, lush land with stream.

DAY ONE
Instruct each child in the following procedures:
❋ Spread Salt Dough onto cardboard base.
❋ Crush foil to form volcano, leaving hole in top (sketch a). Set on base.
❋ Cover foil volcano with Salt Dough, molding dough around base to adhere to landscape.
❋ Make an indentation in dough for a stream (sketch b).
❋ Stick several twigs in dough for palm tree trunks.
❋ Allow to dry overnight.

DAY TWO
Instruct each child in the following procedures:
❋ Paint the volcano and the base around the volcano brown and black.

❋ Paint the remaining flat land green.

DAY THREE
Instruct each child in the following procedures:
❋ Glue black gravel around volcano base and along the stream banks.
❋ Cut several squares of red and orange cellophane in various sizes. Lay pieces on top of each other, bottom edges even.
❋ Tightly twist the bottom of pieces together and wrap tape around base. Insert into volcano opening, gluing in place (sketch c).
❋ Cut green construction paper into four-leaf shapes and glue onto twigs to make palm trees (sketch d).
❋ Gather small pieces of tissue paper into clumps or scrunch into balls to form grass, bushes and other vegetation. Glue onto landscape.
❋ Cut blue plastic wrap to fit stream. Glue onto stream.
❋ With spoons, spread red Soap Dough around top of volcano and let drip down to make lava (sketch e).

Pilot Briefing: **What comes out of a volcano during an eruption?** (Molten lava, ash, gas.) **Some volcanoes emit poisonous gases. But usually volcanic gases are just water, carbon dioxide and sulphur dioxide. The gas smells like rotten eggs, but is harmless.**

a. hole in center

b. twigs

c. glue

d. construction paper — twig

e. red soap dough for lava

tissue paper

blue plastic wrap

Ocean Region (3-D Map)

(For materials and preparation see p. 63.)

LANDSCAPE FEATURES:
A sandy shoreline sloping to the ocean surface.

DAY ONE
Instruct each child in the following procedures:
❀ Spread a layer of Salt Dough onto cardboard base.
❀ Build a curved shoreline on one side of map. Make shore slope to the ocean surface (sketch a).
❀ With dough, form breaking waves and swells in ocean.
❀ Form several dolphins out of dough. Form just the top half or a portion of each dolphin to later glue to the ocean surface (sketch b).
❀ Form the top portion of a whale.
❀ Stick two or three toothpicks in the shore for beach umbrella poles.
❀ Allow molded figures to dry separately from map overnight.

DAY TWO
Instruct each child in the following procedures:
❀ With paintbrush, brush the shore with glue.
❀ Place base in large box and use cup to sprinkle sand onto glued areas. Shake off excess sand into box.
❀ Paint ocean blue and green, blending colors.

❀ Paint dolphins grey.
❀ Paint whale grey, black or blue.

DAY THREE
Instruct each child in the following procedures:
❀ Glue twigs as driftwood onto the shore.
❀ To make beach umbrellas, cut circles out of construction paper then cut a slit half way through each circle (sketch c).
❀ Overlap cut edges slightly and glue. Then glue to toothpicks on shore.
❀ Cut small rectangles out of construction paper and bend in half to make small beach chairs. Cut out construction paper beach towels, surfboards, etc. Decorate items as desired with felt pens and glue onto shore.
❀ Cut a small rectangular piece of construction paper. Fold in half lengthwise and cut off corners (sketch d). Glue sides together to make a boat.
❀ Cut out a construction paper triangle and glue onto a toothpick for a sail. Glue sail onto boat.
❀ Glue boat, dolphins and whale onto ocean.
❀ Dot Soap Dough onto ocean for white caps and onto waves as foam.

Pilot Briefing: **What are most balloons filled with? (Hot air.) Some aeronauts use helium-filled balloons instead of hot air balloons for long journeys. One balloon, called the Double Eagle II, was the first helium balloon to cross the Atlantic Ocean. Seventeen other balloonists had tried to cross the ocean but failed. Some of these balloons had landed in the ocean. So the adventurous pilots of the Double Eagle II had their balloon basket (or gondola) made to float like a boat, in case they had an unfortunate landing in the water.**

a.

sloping shore

b.

whale

Dolphins

c.

cut

glue

d.

cut corners

glue corners

Arctic Region (3-D Map)

(For materials and preparation see p. 63.)

LANDSCAPE FEATURES:
Flat icy land with frozen lake, glaciers and icebergs.

DAY ONE
Instruct each child in the following procedures:
❀ With felt pen, draw the shape of a lake on transparency. Cut out.
❀ Cut a square of foil a little larger than the lake. Glue to the base.
❀ Dot rubber cement onto plastic lake and glue onto foil (sketch a).
❀ Spread Salt Dough onto base, around lake.
❀ Build glaciers out of foil and cover with dough.
❀ Glue together sugar cubes to form igloos (sketch b).
❀ Allow to dry overnight.

DAY TWO
Instruct each child in the following procedures:
❀ Paint flat land white.
❀ Paint mountains and glaciers white, pink or blue

DAY THREE
Instruct each child in the following procedures:
❀ Spoon Soap Dough onto landscape and with a knife, spread over flat surface.
❀ Sprinkle glitter over wet Snow Dough.
❀ Set igloos onto wet landscape.
❀ Cut a small rectangular piece of orange construction paper. Fold in half lengthwise and cut off corners (sketch c). Glue sides to make a canoe.
❀ Break Styrofoam into pieces and glue onto lake as icebergs.

Pilot Briefing: **Glaciers are created in the high mountains where the temperature is so cold that the snow on the ground never melts before more snow falls. When the glacier has grown to the height of a ten-story building, it slowly starts to move down the mountain. How fast do you think a glacier moves?** (Most glaciers move less than three feet a day.) **What do you think happens to the glacier as it moves down the mountain?** (It starts to melt because of warmer temperatures. Eventually it becomes lakes and rivers.)

a. glue transparency onto foil

b. sugar cubes

c. cut off end
fold
glue sides

68

Reproducible Pages

Bible Memory Verse Coloring Posters

The following pages are reproducible and contain 5 Bible Memory Verse designs for younger elementary children and 5 for older elementary children. Ideas for using these pages include:

1. Use the photocopied pages as awards for children who memorize the Bible verse. They may take the page home to color and display.

2. Photocopy a set of coloring posters for each student. Cover with a folded sheet of construction paper and staple to make a coloring book.

3. To customize pages, cover the Bible verse with white paper and letter another verse or saying in its place before you photocopy.

Faith Catcher and Lofty Bird Puppet

1. Photocopy the Faith Catcher Pattern and instructions for each child. Children may color and assemble them if they finish an activity early. Faith Catchers are great take-along games to keep students occupied at transition times.

2. Use the Lofty Bird Puppet Patterns to make your own Lofty Bird for Prekindergarten and Kindergarten children to enjoy.

Student Certificates and Awards

The awards and certificates on the following pages may be personalized for various uses. Just follow these simple procedures:

1. Tear out certificate and letter the name of your program on the appropriate line.

2. Photocopy as many copies of certificate as needed.

3. Letter each child's certificate with his or her name (and achievement when appropriate).

Sticker Posters

1. Photocopy a sticker poster for each student.

2. After students color posters, attach them to a wall or bulletin board.

3. Students add stickers to their posters each day as they arrive. Or you may want to use stickers as rewards for reciting Bible memory verses, being helpful, or completing assignments.

Faith Catcher

(10-15 MINUTES)

This folded paper game will keep children occupied while waiting for a lesson to start or in between planned activities. Not only will your students have fun interacting with each other, but they will learn and memorize what God's Word says about faith!

Materials: Faith Catcher Pattern, photocopier, white copier paper, scissors, colored felt pens.

Preparation: Photocopy pattern onto white paper—one for each child.

Instruct each child in the following procedures:

❀ Cut out Faith Catcher Pattern on solid line.

❀ Color each balloon with a different color felt pen.

❀ Lay paper printed side down.

❀ Fold Faith Catcher in half on dotted line. Open the paper.

❀ Fold paper in half in the opposite direction. Open the paper (sketch a).

❀ Fold paper corners to the middle of back side of paper on dotted lines (sketch b).

❀ Turn folded paper over and fold paper corners into the middle of square on dotted lines (sketch c).

❀ Fold paper in half. Open and fold in half in the opposite direction (sketch d).

❀ Slip your thumbs and pointer fingers into the folded pockets of the game (sketch e).

❀ Move your fingers back and forth and side to side to make the game open and close.

To play game with a partner:

1. Place Faith Catcher on fingers and ask partner to pick a colored balloon.

2. Spell the color name while moving the catcher open for each letter. The catcher should remain open.

3. Have partner choose one of four words of faith. Open and close the catcher to spell out the word.

4. Partner chooses another word of faith. Take the catcher off fingers and open to read the verse printed under the word.

5. Play the game again, this time letting your partner move the catcher.

6. After playing several times, see if you can say the verse under the flaps without looking at them!

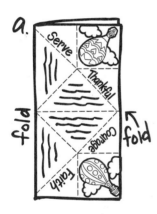

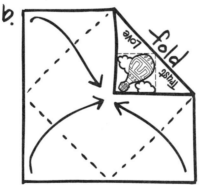

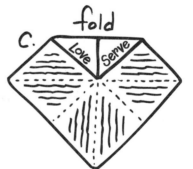

Faith Catcher Pattern

Love

Serve

"The only thing that counts is faith expressing itself through love." Galatians 5:6

"Do not be afraid...do not turn away from the Lord, but serve the Lord with all your heart." 1 Samuel 12:20

Trust

Thankful

"And we know that in all things God works for the good of those who love him, who have been called according to his purpose." Romans 8:28

"Just as you received Christ Jesus as Lord, continue to live in him, rooted and built up in him, strengthened in the faith as you were taught, and overflowing with thankfulness." Colossians 2:6,7

"Trust in the Lord and do good. Commit your way to the Lord." Psalm 37:3,5

"Be strong and courageous. Do not be afraid...for the Lord your God goes with you; he will never leave you nor forsake you." Deuteronomy 31:6

Do Good

Courage

"For God so loved the world that he gave his one and only Son, that whoever believes in him shall not perish but have eternal life." John 3:16

"Now faith is being sure of what we hope for and certain of what we do not see." Hebrews 11:1

Believe

Faith

Lofty Bird Puppet

(15-20 MINUTES)

Materials: A lunch-size paper bag, Bird Patterns, yellow and white card stock, photocopier, colored feathers, felt pens or crayons, glue, scissors

Procedure: Photocopy Head, Claws, Tail and Wing Patterns onto white card stock. Photocopy Beak Patterns onto yellow card stock. Cut out Use felt pens or crayons to color cutouts. Glue feathers onto head, wings and tail as desired. Glue head to flap of paper bag. Bend Beak Patterns on fold lines and glue into place (sketch a). Glue claws to the bottom edge of bag. Glue wings to the inside fold of the bag sides (see sketch b). Fold tab on tail and glue to back of paper bag. Optional—Glue feathers to cover paper bag.

Bird Head
Pattern

Glue beak here.

Bottom Beak Pattern

Top Beak Pattern

Claw Patterns

75

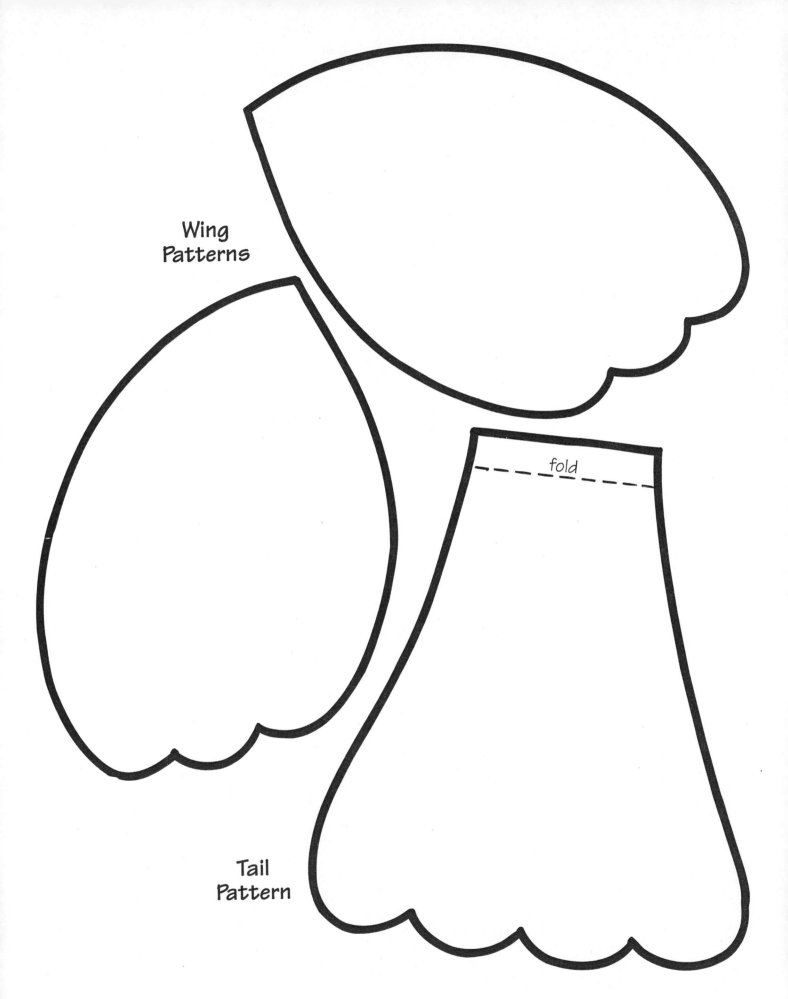

Wing
Patterns

Tail
Pattern

fold

"Be strong and courageous.
Do not be afraid...for the Lord
your God goes with you."
Deuteronomy 31:6

"Trust in the Lord and do good." Psalm 37:3

"The only thing that counts is faith expressing itself through love." Galatians 5:6

The balloon flew higher and higher

"For God so loved the world that he gave his one and only Son, that whoever believes in him shall not perish but have eternal life." John 3:16

Trust in the Lord and do good. Commit your way to the Lord. Psalm 37:3,5

"Do not be afraid... do not turn away from the Lord, but serve the Lord with all your heart." 1 Samuel 12:20

Faith

"The only thing that counts is faith expressing itself through love." Galatians 5:6

"For God so loved the world that he gave his one and only Son, that whoever believes in him shall not perish but have eternal life."
John 3:16

This is to certify that

_____

memorized all the Bible
Memory Verses at

_____

_____

thanks for flying with us at

_____

Friendly Flier Award

_____

was a good friend at

_____

_____

_____

Visitor Award

_____

we're glad you came to
our balloonfest at

_____

Please come back again!

thanks for being a part
of our balloon crew.

This special award
is given to

for

Attendance Award

Presented to

for attendance at

Flight Log

On my adventure today, I learned about...

Elisha

Place sticker here.

Moses

Place sticker here.

Place sticker here.

Jonah

Shadrach Meshach and Abednego

Place sticker here.

Jesus

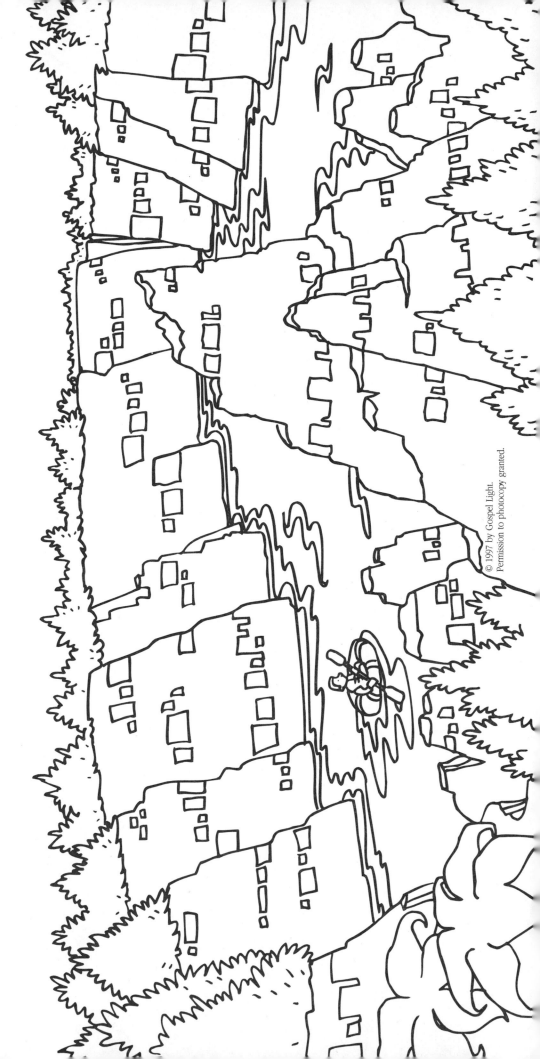

Canyon Sticker Poster

Swamp Sticker Poster

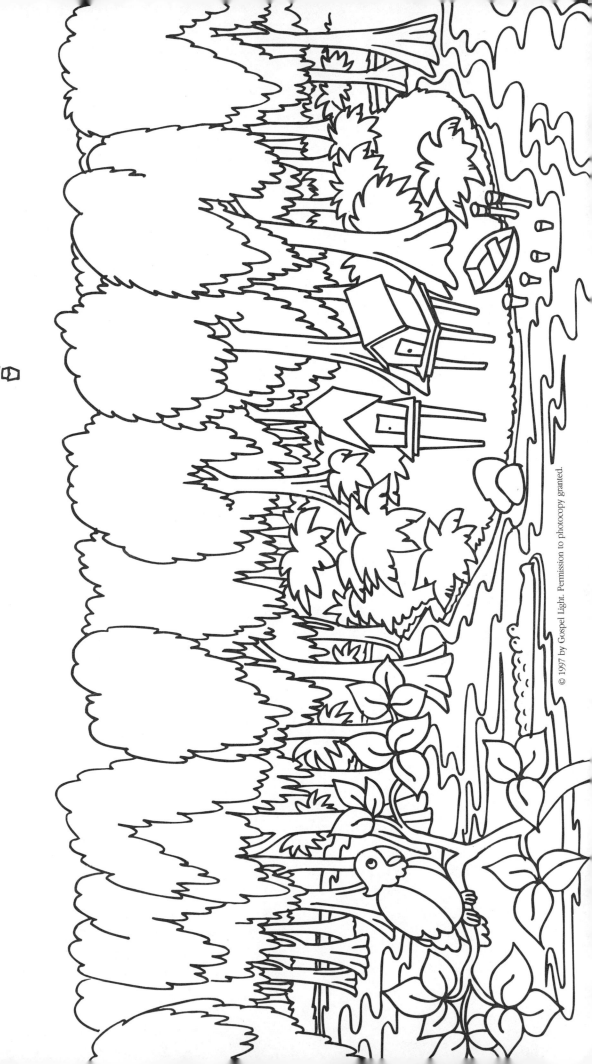

Volcano Sticker Poster

Ocean Sticker Poster

Arctic Sticker Poster

© 1997 by Gospel Light. Permission to photocopy granted.

Index

NOTES